THE DOCTOR'S TRAVEL JOURNAL

*Miracles Around
the World*

By

RICHARD PAUL BARTLETT M.D.

The Doctor's Travel Journal
Miracles Around the World
Richard Paul Bartlett M.D. © 2020

Cover and Interior Design by Fusion Creative Works, FusionCW.com
Cover Design Credit: Mirko Pohle

Hardcover ISBN: 978-1-61206-209-9
Softcover ISBN: 978-1-61206-210-5
eBook ISBN: 978-1-61206-211-2

Published by RB Productions

Printed in the United States of America

Contents

Foreword

There is a difference between a Good idea and a God idea. Good ideas may come to pass; God ideas *will* come to pass. Such are the journeys of Dr. Richard Paul Bartlett. In my opinion, he is the modern-day Doctor Luke of the New Testament. He is a man who clearly hears from God and has decided to use his occupation and his calling to change the lives of others.

This exciting book will take you on the missionary journeys of a man whose steps are ordered by the Lord. As you read, you will encounter the obstacles he faced, and see how God gave him the inspiration and wisdom to work through life-threatening danger and make decisions when his family's livelihood or his professional reputation hung in the balance. You will live the challenging moments, which at times looked overwhelming, and grasp how God provided miracles. This book brings the recognition of what awaits you on the other side of your obedience to God ideas.

Pastor Tim Storey

Introduction

Landslide!

June 11, 2015
Nepal

Clouds of dust were swirling from way up the mountain as several boulders came tumbling down in front of us. What a beautiful day! Wispy white clouds, like feathers in the blue sky, floated above the rugged Himalayan Mountains surrounding us. The dirt road in front of us was not impassable—yet. The landslide had slowed for a moment.

Our medical mission team had been in Nepal for over a week. It was surreal that I was in the Himalayas after three major earthquakes. Tremors and aftershocks had punctuated our trip to Nepal. Whole mountainsides were sliding into the Class V rapids that roared alongside the mountain roads.

And now the mission was completed. I just needed to get back to Kathmandu to catch my flight home. There was just one problem . . . a new landslide in front of me across the only road to Kathmandu.

Looking down the treacherous mountain, the white-water rapids swirled and foamed below. There were no guardrails or precautions along the cliffside roads. On the other side of the mound of fresh rocks and dirt, blocking the road, was the remainder of the mission team, standing next to two SUVs. The Nepali teenaged SUV drivers refused to drive across for fear of a boulder bounding down and erasing the SUV from the mountainside. I couldn't blame them after all the destruction we had seen during this trip. I'd been to the Iraqi war zone, and most buildings were still standing there. In Nepal, there were no buildings left standing in many of the villages. Two-story buildings were reduced to piles of brick, dust, and concrete fragments on both sides of the roads, miles of pure destruction. We witnessed people walking on top of rubble that used to be homes and businesses, searching for anything of value.

Now it was time to leave Nepal. We just needed to get to the SUVs on the other side of this landslide before it was too late. Looking across the fresh rocks and dirt, the rest of mission team by the SUVs seemed so far away. Most had their cell phones pointed at the four of us, taking videos and pictures. A 22-year-old Nepali college soccer player had joined Dilip, Kurt, and me to translate for the clinic for the last several days. Kurt Gorton, a sturdy missionary and roofing contractor from Arkansas had stayed behind in the remote village to help me with the last clinic. Dilip Thapa, a pudgy, local Nepali pastor, had been our translator for the whole trip. He was always quick to smile.

Back to the immediate problem—the landslide. The rest of the team was far out of earshot. It was up to the two Nepali men, Kurt, and me, to decide our fate.

"I guess we can make a run for it when the falling rocks slow for a moment," I stated. Dilip frowned.

Kurt said, "I'm not worried. Let's do this."

And that is how easy it is to make potentially life-ending decisions. Four men; no lady in the group to slow us down with common sense or good judgment. We grabbed our luggage and before I could muster the courage, the soccer star was off, racing toward the landslide, holding his suitcase over his head. Like a mountain goat, he agilely bounded onto the rubble, righting himself after a stumble. He sprinted to our waiting team and was swallowed in group hugs on the other side of the landslide. That was the craziest 100-yard dash I had ever seen.

INTRODUCTION

I readied myself and thought, *Here goes nothing. Or everything!* I decided if I ran fast I would be in harm's way for less time. I sprinted with an oversized suitcase in my left hand. I kept my eyes locked straight ahead. I purposefully avoided looking up at the mountain.

I had been running on the treadmill back home fairly regularly. Now I was running for my life! I could only imagine the football-sized rocks flying over my head. It felt like my feet were barely touching the ground; I felt like I was flying!

Is this really necessary on my birthday? I thought. *Yes, my epitaph would be unique: same birth and death dates and death by landslide in the Himalayan Mountains!*

How did I get in this situation? Let me start at the beginning.

CHAPTER 1

Called to Nepal

After Iraq

In February 2015, I was at home in Texas. It had been several months since I had come home from a medical mission to Duhok, Iraq. I had witnessed miracles God was doing despite ISIS and could not stop talking about it. Naïvely, I assumed every Christian would be excited to hear about miracles Jesus was doing in the present day. Any pastor that was willing to listen was going to hear what God did right under the nose of ISIS. I was just so amazed, as were many others.

Russ Nebhut, the new pastor of Asbury Methodist Church in Odessa, rented a place downtown for me to speak. He promoted the event for people to come, free of charge, and hear me speak about my experience. I was gung-ho to tell people about God's works. I also had the privilege to speak at two Sunday school classes at Odessa First Baptist church. Pastor Don Caywood allowed me to report what I saw to the entire congregation of Odessa Christian Faith Center. The place was packed. I was invited to speak at Midland's First Baptist Men's prayer meeting.

KCRS 550AM, the number one talk-radio station in West Texas, invited me to take 15 minutes of their morning show to talk about my experience. It went well. For many of the listeners it was the first time they'd heard that everyone in the Middle East was not the same.

I pointed out that the Kurds are allies with the U.S., fighting ISIS, and we should support them. At that point, no one was talking about the Kurds. It was a new thing to promote that message in America.

Matthew 13:24-30 NIV:

> Jesus told them another parable: "The kingdom of heaven is like a man who sowed good seed in his field. But while everyone was sleeping, his enemy came and sowed weeds among the wheat, and went away. When the wheat sprouted and formed heads, then the weeds also appeared.
>
> "The owner's servants came to him and said, 'Sir, didn't you sow good seed in your field? Where then did the weeds come from?'
>
> "'An enemy did this,' he replied.
>
> "The servants asked him, 'Do you want us to go and pull them up?'
>
> "'No,' he answered, 'because while you are pulling the weeds, you may uproot the wheat with them. Let both grow together until the harvest. At that time I will tell the harvesters: First collect the weeds and tie them in bundles to be burned; then gather the wheat and bring it into my barn.'"

Wolves in Shepherd's (Pastor's) Clothing

Also in February, a former pastor of a traditional mega-church in Midland, Texas, had just gotten back from the Middle East. A patient of mine was a member of that congregation. She knew I had recently returned from a mission to Iraq. She told me the pastor would be speaking about his trip and she encouraged me to come. She said I should speak as well.

I got to the church an hour early because I was so excited about what I had seen Jesus do in Iraq—He had kept His word, as He told in Mark 16:15-18.

It was a packed evening meeting at the church. I saw Mike Conaway, the Midland U.S. congressman, seated at the back. U.S. Congressman

CALLED TO NEPAL

Frank Wolf joined the pastor as he spoke about their new creation: an organization promoting religious freedom, even for those without religious faith. The pastor spoke about the need for religious freedom in Iraq. (This is a very different goal than evangelism!) Rape, murder, and theft were occurring in Syria and Iraq because of many acting "freely" on their "religious beliefs" from the Koran. After the pastor finished, he asked the audience for questions and comments.

After several questions, I stood up and was handed a microphone. In front of hundreds of people, I told them that I was recently in Iraq. I told them how I saw amazing things that God is doing. I said I saw people delivered from demons, people healed during prayer, and Muslim people becoming Christians.

The pastor quickly grabbed the microphone away and, looking at the crowd, he snarked, "I've been trying to cast demons out of my deacons for years!" Laughter.

At that very moment, the pastor's friend, David Pierce, was serving his sixth year in an Arkansas prison. He and Pierce were leaders together of a church in Benton, Arkansas, from 1984–1988. He did not report or remove Pierce from leadership. After this pastor left Benton, Pierce was charged with 54 counts of sexual indecency with church children. Little boys. This was reported in the *Benton Courier*, August 27, 2009.

Matthew 18:3-20 NIV:
And he said: "Truly I tell you, unless you change and become like little children, you will never enter the kingdom of heaven. Therefore, whoever takes the lowly position of this child is the greatest in the kingdom of heaven. And whoever welcomes one such child in my name welcomes me.

"If anyone causes one of these little ones—those who believe in me—to stumble, it would be better for them to have a large millstone hung around their neck and to be drowned in the depths of the sea. Woe to the world because of the things that cause people to stumble! Such things must come, but woe to the person through whom they come! If your hand or your foot causes you to stumble, cut it off and throw it away. It is better for you to enter life maimed or crippled than to have two hands or two feet and be thrown into eternal fire. And if your eye causes you to stumble, gouge it out and throw it away. It is better for you to enter life with one eye than to have two eyes and be thrown into the fire of hell.

"See that you do not despise one of these little ones. For I tell you that their angels in heaven always see the face of my Father in heaven.

"What do you think? If a man owns a hundred sheep, and one of them wanders away, will he not leave the ninety-nine on the hills and go to look for the one that wandered off? And if he finds it, truly I tell you, he is happier about that one sheep than about the ninety-nine that did not wander off. In the same way your Father in heaven is not willing that any of these little ones should perish.

"If your brother or sister sins, go and point out their fault, just between the two of you. If they listen to you, you have won them over. But if they will not listen, take one or two others along, so that 'every matter may be established by the testimony of two or three witnesses.' If they still refuse to listen, tell it to the church; and if they refuse to listen even to the church, treat them as you would a pagan or a tax collector.

"Truly I tell you, whatever you bind on earth will be bound in heaven, and whatever you loose on earth will be loosed in heaven.

"Again, truly I tell you that if two of you on earth agree about anything they ask for, it will be done for them by my Father in heaven."

This is no laughing matter. According to retired Texas appellate attorney Christa Brown, author of *This Little Light: Beyond a Baptist Preacher Predator and his Gang* (Foremost Press, 2009), this is a count of child predators who were active in church or school leadership, by state (see Appendix I for more details):

- Alabama: 6

- Arkansas: 5

- Florida: 13

- Kentucky: 9

- Missouri: 7

- Oklahoma: 8

- South Carolina: 7

- Texas: 33

Christa's book is available on Amazon. Every large denomination will have wolves in sheep's clothing slip in, but how will the denomination deal with the problem? Will they protect the predators or the children?

Ephesians 5:11-12 NIV:
"Have nothing to do with the fruitless deeds of darkness, but rather expose them. It is shameful even to mention what the disobedient do in secret."

Acts 20:29 NKJV:
For I know this, that after my departure savage wolves will come in among you, not sparing the flock.

Luke 10:3 NKJV:
Go your way; behold, I send you out as lambs among wolves.

Matthew 7:15-23 NKJV:
"Beware of false prophets, who come to you in sheep's clothing, but inwardly they are ravenous wolves. You will know them by their fruits. Do men gather grapes from thornbushes or figs from thistles? Even so, every good tree bears good fruit, but a bad tree bears bad

fruit. A good tree cannot bear bad fruit, nor can a bad tree bear good fruit. Every tree that does not bear good fruit is cut down and thrown into the fire. Therefore by their fruits you will know them.

"Not everyone who says to Me, 'Lord, Lord,' shall enter the kingdom of heaven, but he who does the will of My Father in heaven. Many will say to Me in that day, 'Lord, Lord, have we not prophesied in Your name, cast out demons in Your name, and done many wonders in Your name?' And then I will declare to them, 'I never knew you; depart from Me, you who practice lawlessness!'"

Still, day after day, I couldn't stop speaking about what I had seen Jesus do in Iraq.

Iraqi Demon Possession

On March 12 of 2019, *BBC News* had a story titled "Germany murder: Iraqi admits Wiesbaden teenager killing." In the article the murderer, Ali Bashar, was 22 at the time of the trial. He admitted to strangling a 15-year-old girl named Susana Feldman but he says he did not know how it happened. In the article he said, "Everything went black before my eyes, then it all happened." The defendant told the court, through an interpreter, "I don't know how it could have happened." Ali Bashar was also accused of attacking a man in a park and raping an 11-year-old girl, all while he was in Germany (https://www.bbc.com/news/world-europe-47536431).

Ali and his family came to Germany as refugees in 2015. After several years they returned to Iraq. After the murders, the head of the German Federal Police, Dieter Romann, took a SWAT team and an anti-terror police team with him to Irbil, Iraq. They snatched Ali Bashar and extradited him back to Germany for trial. They did that despite the fact that Iraq and Germany do not have an extradition treaty.

Obviously, what he described fit perfectly with demon possession. The demon took over and committed rape and murder. Numerous serial killers and rapists give similar accounts in the mainstream media. A January 13, 2020, *BBC News* article titled "Drug-binge man who murdered stranger in his own home jailed" had the same pattern (https://www.bbc.com/news/uk-scotland-north-east-orkney-shetland-51090398). That happened in the United Kingdom. In Iraq, Thailand, and Serbia, I witnessed people freed from the same problem in Jesus' name.

Luke 12:1-12 NIV:

> Meanwhile, when a crowd of many thousands had gathered, so that they were trampling on one another, Jesus began to speak first to his disciples, saying: "Be on your guard against the yeast of the Pharisees, which is hypocrisy. There is nothing concealed that will not be disclosed, or hidden that will not be made known. What you have said in the dark will be heard in the daylight, and what you have whispered in the ear in the inner rooms will be proclaimed from the roofs.

> "I tell you, my friends, do not be afraid of those who kill the body and after that can do no more. But I will show you whom you should fear: Fear him who, after your body has been killed, has authority to throw you into hell. Yes, I tell you, fear him. Are not five sparrows sold for two pennies? Yet not one of them is forgotten by God. Indeed, the very hairs of your head are all numbered. Don't be afraid; you are worth more than many sparrows.

> "I tell you, whoever publicly acknowledges me before others, the Son of Man will also acknowledge before the angels of God. But whoever disowns me before others will be disowned before the angels of God. And everyone who speaks a word against the Son of Man will be forgiven, but anyone who blasphemes against the Holy Spirit will not be forgiven.

> "When you are brought before synagogues, rulers and authorities, do not worry about how you will defend yourselves or what you

will say, for the Holy Spirit will teach you at that time what you should say."

ISIS Update

BBC News published an article on March 6, 2019, titled "IS militants caught trying to escape last Syria enclave." The article described the final remnant of ISIS in one small town called Baghuz in Syria. (https://www.bbc.com/news/world-middle-east-47468228)

The town was surrounded by the Kurds and the Syrian Democratic Forces. So both Syrian soldiers and Kurdish soldiers surrounded the village. The United States, of course, was also involved in supporting the defeat of ISIS. The citizens in that village were allowed to leave peacefully and they found ISIS soldiers trying to escape with the civilians, posing as local peasants.

The article summarized the story of ISIS. On January 10, 2006, the group announced the Islamic State of Iraq and Abu Bakr al-Baghdadi became its leader. On January 1, 2013, they seized control of a territory in Syria. ISIS stood for the Islamic State in Iraq and Syria. In January 2014, ISIS conquered over a dozen Iraqi cities, including Mosul and Tikrit. ISIS seized Syria's largest oilfield in Homs province. Al-Baghdadi moved to Mosul, the Iraq ISIS headquarters. He was 30 miles down the road from our medical mission in Duhok, Iraq for 10 days.

On June 29, the jihadist group declared the creation of a caliphate. On January 8, 2014, ISIS fighters began killing and enslaving thousands of people and releasing videos of Western hostages being beheaded. On January 9, the US began airstrikes on the Syrian ISIS capital of Raqqa. By January 1, 2015, Isis was at the height of its control over eight million people and over 34,000 square miles of western Syria and eastern Iraq. ISIS generated billions of dollars from oil, extortion, kidnapping, and robbery.

On January 3, 2016, the Syrian government recaptured Palmyra but lost it again in December of 2016. They recaptured the UNESCO

World Heritage site in March of 2017. That site was the remnants of a temple to Baal. The UN celebrated preserving a temple to Baal.

On January 7, 2017, Iraqi forces liberated Mosul, and the 10-month battle left thousands of civilians dead. More than 800,000 people were displaced when most of the city was destroyed. President Trump was at a factory in Ohio that makes the A1 Abrams tank, on March 20, 2019. He announced that there was no more ISIS in Syria or Iraq.

President Trump announced on October 27, 2019, that ISIS leader al-Baghdadi detonated a suicide belt, killing himself and three children. A special forces operation cornered al-Baghdadi in a dead-end tunnel under a compound in Syria. "Last night the United States brought the world's number one terrorist leader to justice. He died like a dog. He died like a coward. The world is now a much safer place. He was a sick and depraved man, and now he's gone," said President Trump.

Spontaneous Plan

On a morning in May 2015, I had arrived before sunrise at my medical office in West Texas. Waiting for the staff to arrive, I turned on the computer and checked the World Missions Alliance website. I noticed an upcoming mission to Nepal in 10 days. I didn't know much about Nepal. I had never felt a draw to go there until that moment.

I called Chuck Todd, President of World Missions Alliance. Chuck has been leading missionary projects in the "hot spots" of the world since 1990. I told him I was looking at the Nepal mission, but it was probably too late to join. He said "Actually, someone just dropped out today. There is an opening if you want to come!" I made sure Chuck knew I couldn't commit to anything without talking to my wife.

Chuck said this trip had been scheduled for a year. They had no idea that three major earthquakes would happen just before the trip. Nepal was completely devastated. The third earthquake killed over 9,000 and injured more than 20,000. Eighty percent of the population were now homeless in the entire nation. Chuck said that, in Nepal, a big church is 100 people, counting children. A local pastor, Reuben, got 18 pastors in the country of Nepal to work together to help our team with translation, transportation, and logistics. Chuck said pastors working together on this scale had never happened before in Nepal.

Everything Falls in Place

I did not expect that telling my wife I wanted to lead a medical mission to Nepal in less than two weeks would go well. My medical mission to Iraq had been such an emotional roller coaster for my family. Chuck and Helen Todd and I were interviewed by the ABC, CBS, and NBC local news affiliates before we left for Iraq. We had become a spectacle in West Texas before we left. Everyone wanted to know why we would be stupid enough to go to Iraq in November 2014. ISIS was in the news every evening. My family was still recovering emotionally.

My wife was not excited that I wanted to lead a medical mission to Nepal, but she told me that if I felt the Lord was leading me, then I should go. I called Chuck, who then connected me to his staff member who scheduled the plane tickets for the mission teams. She quoted a ticket price that was ridiculously cheap. I thought, *Well, I can do that!*

While I was on the phone, she said, "The price just got even cheaper!"

In retrospect, who would want to fly to Nepal shortly after *three major earthquakes?* Of course the ticket demand and prices were low.

In my absence, would someone cover my regular clinic where I care for employees for an oil company? I called a nurse practitioner friend and she agreed to cover my clinic. I called to bounce it off the human resources head of the oil company.

She said, "What kind of human would I be if I told you not to go help those poor people in Nepal after they had three earthquakes?"

Within half a day everything had fallen into place. I called my friend Danny Skaggs, a pharmacist. I told him I was going to do a medical mission in Nepal. Danny offered to donate the medicine. I was shocked that everything came together so quickly. If you were to have asked me that morning, I would've had no idea that I'd be in Nepal 10 days later.

Perfect Timing

June 2015, Kathmandu, Nepal: Tall buildings of concrete with laundry hanging from windows and roofs, surrounded by the breathtaking Himalayas, were my first sights from our hotel. Chuck gathered the mission team to introduce the local pastors who would translate for our medical clinics and coordinate travel and logistics for the trip. Pastor Reuben explained that if we had come any sooner, he would not have been able to help us because they were still digging people out of the rubble. However, if we had come any later, the monsoons were expected to cause mudslides, washing the roads off the mountainsides due to instability caused by the earthquakes. It was a narrow window of opportunity. There was no commerce—no place to buy food, no place to make money. Shelves were bare at pharmacies and most grocery stores. It was just like the end of the world for them. It was End-Time devastation.

Most of the people had left their cities, villages, and family farms to go to the capital city and live in donated tents. They waited for daily rations of food and water. No medical care was available. Sprawling, overcrowded tent cities covered open fields outside Kathmandu, the capital city. We heard that rape and theft were common, with families forced to share a tent with 30 strangers in tent cities. Criminals mixed freely with the general public.

Gautama, the guy they called Buddha, was believed to have been born in Nepal. Nepal is a land with thousands of years of false gods. There were idols and altars everywhere. The Hindu religion was the only religion governmentally promoted and encouraged until 2007; there was an iron fist holding the country spiritually. The earthquakes shook it open. The government was financially overwhelmed and open to any help they could get. We were able to provide free food, blankets, and medical care, and share the Gospel unhindered.

I met Dilip during breakfast. He explained that when he was a young man, he came to Kathmandu to learn to be a movie director. At school he met a young lady who was studying to be an actress. They got married. After they were married, his wife became very ill. Christians prayed for her and she was healed; it was miraculous. Dilip was raised as a Buddhist, but after he saw Jesus heal his wife, he and his wife became Christians.

Later, Dilip became a pastor and he started bringing copies of *The Jesus Film* (the 1979 film starring Brian Deacon and directed by Peter Sykes and John Krish, and produced by John Heyman) up into the remote villages of Nepal. They would sometimes walk 18 hours through the mountains, with a projector, screen, generator, and other equipment on their backs. In those remote villages, they would set up a tent for a night showing of the movie for crowds consisting of, at the most, a few hundred people. Most of the people had never heard of Jesus Christ or Christianity. He recalled to me about one village where half of the people became Christians right after the movie showing.

From One Extreme to Another

Dilip told me about another occasion when they had packed up the mountain into a remote village to show *The Jesus Film*. A little boy in the village started screaming and acting up every time Dilip, or one of his team members, came close to him. Dilip asked the child's parents if they would allow him to pray for their child. They agreed, hastily, and said that the boy had been out of control for years, getting more and more bizarre in his behavior. They told Dilip their son had started killing chickens and drinking their blood. They were desperate for help. Dilip and his friends prayed for that little 10-year-old boy. Jesus delivered the boy from demons. That was eight years ago and now the young boy is the pastor of a fledgling church in that village.

Holy Cow?

We loaded in SUVs to go to the church in Kathmandu where Reuben pastored. Trucks, cars, motorcycles, and tuk tuks (a sort of auto rickshaw for transporting several people) all dodged cattle that were walking unfettered through six lanes of traffic.

I knew the Hindu idea of reincarnation believed that cows might be deceased family members. Dilip explained that cows serve another purpose within their caste system. Satan changes the definition of words, such as "holy." Cows are part of the religious system: when you are of a higher caste level and you are touched by someone of a lower caste level, you become "unclean," according to Hindu belief. To become "clean and holy" again, you must anoint your head with cow urine and drink cow urine, thus the need for cows everywhere.

We saw altars to false gods in the middle of cornfields, in the middle of city streets, and in the middle of highways. Dilip said we would drive past the largest statue of Shiva, the god of destruction, on a mountainside every day as we made our way to the villages.

False Gods

Reuben explained that in Hinduism there are 360,000 gods and counting. If they hear of another one, they add it to the list and build a shrine where the new false god was allegedly seen. God is a God of order; Satan is the author of confusion. The shrines in the middle of crop fields, highways, and busy roads were very disruptive. Everywhere someone thought they saw a god, they built a shrine to it. They really might have seen something; we know that a third of the angels fell, so there are sometimes manifestations.

Enlightenment

In Nepal, I realized the people had been stuck in a world without enlightenment for thousands of years. How ironic that people come to Nepal searching for "enlightenment." Jesus came, and was resurrected, and most in Nepal still don't know. The Himalayas are a part of the world that has been almost completely untouched by the Good News. Instead, most have been living in spiritual darkness. They aren't living victorious lives with Jesus as their Lord and Savior; they are living the lives of victims without Christ.

Marijuana

We unloaded to walk a few blocks to a church service on the edge of Kathmandu. Chuck pointed to the 10-foot-tall weeds growing out of the ditches on the sides of the road. When I looked closer, I realized they were marijuana plants growing wild. I hadn't seen anybody using marijuana in any way. Nowhere in Nepal, during the whole trip, did I see anyone using it.

Jesus Still Heals

Day two in Nepal: Our first full-day medical clinic was held in a huge tent donated by China, in a sprawling refugee tent city on the outskirts of Kathmandu. The sun was shining and it was a beautiful morning, hot with no breeze. I resisted the urge to take my white coat and necktie off. Despite being soaked in sweat, I wanted to assure the patients of my role as a doctor.

Patients lined up outside the tent in the heat. The air was filled with chatter and excitement. First, patients were offered prayer by mission members as they waited to be triaged in the tent next to the clinic tent. All patients were receptive to prayer. Team members presented the Gospel with translators. A few times, everyone in the tent who was waiting to be triaged for the clinic would hear the Gospel and accept Christ, praying in unison. The team passed a lot of Bibles out to people who became Christians.

A dear couple from Arkansas, Kurt and Cindy Gorton, were trained in first aid prior to the trip and were assisting with triage. With translators, they obtained patient histories and vital signs. In my clinic tent, eye contact with patients led to frequent smiles and bows with hands in prayer position. Patients came in the tent carrying their medical triage info on a piece of paper. After greetings, they would sit and tell the translator, either Reuben or his daughter, what was bothering them. I would read the triage notes and a targeted history and physical would follow.

After several hours, I was called outside for an emergency. A boy had collapsed while standing in the heat. We carried him into the tent, praying as we obtained his vital signs, and encouraged him to drink a bottle of water. He recovered quickly. By early afternoon, we had treated many with common urgent care issues. We treated patients quickly because a very long line of patients continued to come.

Wiping the sweat from my brow with my white coat sleeve, I reached for another bottled water. Turning around, I saw a young man, with his right arm hanging limp at his side, in the chair with his triage note. Reuben said, "He is paralyzed from a stroke, Doc. You aren't going to be able to help him." I nodded, looking at my luggage full of meds, stacked in order. None of the meds could help this man. I felt my face flush as I realized our team had let this poor man stand in line in the hot sun, knowing there was no hope medically.

Frustrated, I blurted out, "We can at least pray for him!" Reuben's daughter had their new video camera rolling as everyone else on the team reached out to the man and started praying simultaneously. I unscrewed the cap off the small vial of oil I had retrieved from my coat pocket and turned it upside down on my index finger. I anointed his forehead and started praying.

The thought came to me, *Do a neurologic exam.* I turned to Reuben and said, "Tell him to squeeze my fingers." I held my hands in front of the patient. The 28-year-old man reached both arms toward me. His right hand shook as he wrapped his fingers around my fingers, eyes wide in amazement.

Reuben's daughter said, "God is doing a miracle!"

Facing the patient, I crossed my arms to touch my shoulders. "Tell him to touch his shoulders." Reuben rattled off the orders. I didn't think the young man's eyes could open any wider! He copied my movements, with his right arm shaking.

"Tell him to stand up and walk!" I said and grabbed his hand and he rose up, leaning his right shoulder against my left. I pulled back the tent flap and squinted in the brightness at the crowd blocking the entrance as they waited in line.

The crowd parted as the man limped out beside me, holding my hand. He was leaning heavily on me. We walked between the rows of tents. The crowds parted to either side of us. People stopped to stare. Though he limped, he was no longer leaning on me! His limp was decreasing. His gait was becoming more normal as I continued to thank God, quoting healing Scriptures. I looked at him, and a grin spread across his face from ear to ear and tears streamed down his cheeks.

After 100 yards, we passed the last tents and turned. We walked hand in hand back to the tent. Reuben and a crowd gathered around the man with excited chatter. Reuben introduced three strangers and said they were with the Kathmandu newspaper. They were sent to this refugee camp to find stories to report in tomorrow's paper. I told Reuben to speak with them and his daughter could translate for me in the clinic. I noticed that they interviewed the healed paralytic. A second news team from Kathmandu arrived to interview Reuben and the healed man.

I realized that most of the crowd had never heard of Jesus (Yeshua) or the Good News before. This was their first exposure to the Living God. The clinic continued and I started incorporating prayer into the care I provided for the remainder of the day. Until then, I had relied on the team's prayers and focused totally on providing medical care.

Irritant

A tall, weathered woman with graying blond hair appeared at the entrance of our medical tent. She had her hands on her hips and glared

88986_99062105)

at the people near her. Reuben tapped me on the shoulder and told me someone wanted to talk to me. I approached in my white lab coat and she went on an angry rant against antibiotics in general. Her English was broken; I guessed Europe was her origin. I asked her who she was and what organization she was with. She stood with her mouth open, silent, and seemed to deflate. Apparently she didn't expect to be questioned and wasn't qualified to be judging what we were doing. She turned and stomped out of the tent. She quickly melted into the crowd, not to be seen or heard from again.

Infiltrator

The next morning, after breakfast and prayer, we rode in two vans to a busy bus stop in the middle of the capital. There we picked up the local pastors who translated for us. One of the local pastors had a thin white lady with a British accent standing close to him. The pastor introduced her as someone who was at the bus stop and wanted to join us. She told us she had been looking for a nonprofit organization to join, but she had been denied by all others. She was excited to join us.

Without speaking to each other, three of our mission team got the same bad impression when we first met her. I had a gut feeling that she was trouble. Kurt Gorton from Arkansas told me the Scripture about Nehemiah came to his mind. The Scripture tells of God's people working on a project in unity, and then the enemy would slip in among them and try to discourage God's people to hinder the work. Madeleine Maine from California said she saw a demon when she first looked at the woman. We had not talked to each other yet.

All three of us got the same message from God in three different ways, and by the end of the day it was confirmed. When we arrived at the Christian school courtyard, we set up for the medical clinic. The new woman was constantly interfering with the normal process of things. I was organizing my medication so I could find the right treatments easily during the clinic. She came uncomfortably close to me, speaking louder than normal about various random topics.

Stepping back, I asked her what her past professions had been. She explained that she used to be a nurse. I told her I did not need her help and she had to leave. I am convinced that she lost her nursing license because of a drug problem, and she was tagging along with us to find drugs.

Meeting that woman marked the first of a series of things that began going wrong until the end of the trip. The other two team members and I, who were warned by God about the woman, did not know about each other's messages from God until four days later. Her behavior during the clinic confirmed our impressions. I found out at the end of the day that she had gone through all my bags of medicine. She had also been caught rifling through Kurt's backpack, which had his clinic supplies. A young team member reported that the woman went around mumbling and murmuring; she was definitely not normal. One of our team members heard her mumble to herself that she had come to cause confusion. Over the remaining days, we had a couple of flat tires and a landslide that slowed our progress.

Out of My Comfort Zone

Nepal was thrust upon me at the last minute. I know it was by design that God didn't give me a lot of time to do research. I don't really like heights. It didn't originally register with me that Nepal is located high in the mountains—the land of Mount Everest. After I got there it became clear that I was out of my comfort zone. I'd rather be dealing with militarized zones and thugs with guns than mountains and cliffs. God knew I didn't like high places and that the Himalayan Mountains would not be my happy place. He also knew I was needed there, so I wasn't given time to research and talk myself out of it—a divine need-to-know basis.

Each day we traveled to different remote mountaintop clearings littered with makeshift shelters of tarp, cardboard, and scraps of wood and tin. We unloaded our supplies and provided medical clinics. We traveled outside the city of Kathmandu for hours on one-and-a-half-lane wide dirt roads.

CALLED TO NEPAL

There were no guardrails running along the edges of cliffs in the Himalaya Mountains. The accepted driving culture was to honk while passing vehicles blindly around corners, to let people know you were coming. Honking, the Nepali assumed, gave them the right to barrel around blind corners as fast as they could. Nepali drivers assumed that the person on the other side of the mountain could hear the horn honking and would stay out of the way.

Chuck said cars and buses occasionally went over the cliffs. Four years before, Chuck's team had come across a bus that tumbled down the mountainside. Everyone had died. I had that in the back of my mind the rest of the trip. We had local drivers that were hired to drive the SUVs. They were teenagers who had little Buddha statues on the dash. That didn't give me any confidence that they were hearing from the Lord. They would swerve to dodge a rock in the dirt roads, causing the tires to be on the edge of the cliff.

I thought of the unstable soil from the quakes causing the landslides we had passed as we traveled. What if the ground gave way under the weight of the tires? Reuben noticed my white knuckles as I watched the traffic coming toward us and the sheer cliffs beside us.

Rueben said, "Don't worry, the drivers are professionals." I thought, *Yeah, and I bet the bus driver that drove over the cliff four years ago was a professional too.* I thanked Reuben for trying to calm my nerves. I put in my earphones and listened to Christian music on my iPod while trying to stare toward the mountainside and away from the cliff edge.

There were two occasions, as we drove up a switchback, that the vehicle was not getting traction even though our wheels were spinning. Both times, our vehicle started to roll backward toward the edge of the cliff. Both times, the driver hit the brake and the car slid backward to a stop several feet from disaster. The instant the vehicle stopped moving, I opened the back door and jumped out of the vehicle. My heart was racing before I took the first step.

I called back, "I'll see you at the top!" I just kept running up the mountain until I was out of breath. Due to the thin air, that was only about half of a mile. I then stopped and watched the SUVs slowly wind up the mountain to join me five minutes later. Yes, that happened twice.

Prayer Ribbons

On the way to a remote camp of refugees, we traveled up winding roads with dense forest on both sides. At first, it looked like there was litter caught in the trees, but as we passed it became clear that colored ribbons were tied to the branches. We were told the Buddhists and Hindus would write prayers on those ribbons, and then tie them in the trees. The belief was that when the wind blew across the ribbons, it carried the prayers into the air for the spirits to receive them.

I thought about how it was a close counterfeit to many things that we know from the Bible. John 3:8 tells how Jesus says that the wind blows wherever it pleases, and it is the same way with people who are led by the Holy Spirit. Ephesians 6:18 includes words about praying in the spirit, and in Romans 8:26 it says that the spirit Himself intercedes for us through wordless groaning. I see clearly how, with just a slight twisting of truths, those wordless groanings could be blurred into being the sounds of wind blowing prayers into the air.

Staying Behind

The last two days of clinics were in Kodari, a remote village on the border near Tibet. Kodari was at the epicenter of one of the earthquakes. I could look across the river below to the mountainside, and across to Tibet.

The five-hour SUV ride from Kathmandu was unnerving. The first clinic went well. At the end of the day, I offered to stay in Kodari overnight so I could start the last day of clinics earlier. Otherwise, I would lose five hours returning the next day for clinic; and I would have to endure five extra hours of death-defying road time. That village was where Pastor Dilip was from, and he offered a place for Kurt and me to stay overnight with him at his uncle's empty home. The uncle's home was one of the few concrete homes, hanging on the edge of the roadside cliff overlooking the river below. It appeared undamaged, but I was wary.

Luckily, the home did not slide down the mountain and into the river overnight. We did a morning clinic with just Kurt, Dilip, two other locals, and me. We saw 120 patients in the morning clinic, treating high blood pressure, diabetes, wound infections, ear infections, and more. Twice we heard a rescue helicopter fly overhead, responding to new landslides. When the morning clinic was finished, we walked out of the tent to sit on a curb in the shade. We were hot, sweaty, and exhausted. I was satisfied knowing that I had used all of the meds brought for the mission.

Change of Plans

Dilip's cell phone rang. He hung up and told us Chuck had called. A new landslide had blocked the road, meaning the team could not drive past it to pick us up. I looked at my return airline ticket for the next morning from Kathmandu.

Dilip asked, "What do we do?"

I said, "We aren't going to just sit here. Let's start walking toward Kathmandu and figure this out."

Pastor Dilip, Kurt, and I, along with our helpers, started walking through Kodari back toward Kathmandu. I heard a generator humming louder as we walked through the abandoned streets. We came across an SUV parked on the curb. A generator was outside of one of the few two-story buildings still standing downtown. An electric cord trailed into the open door and I motioned for us to walk inside. Dilip talked in Nepali to the three men inside. He turned to tell me they worked for the city and were trying to restore some utilities for Kodari. Dilip said they were too busy to help us and could not use the city-owned SUV to help us.

I pulled Dilip aside and told him I had $10 U.S. if they could help us. At that point, the boss realized he could give us a ride to the landslide while the other two kept working on the utilities. We loaded up, grinning at each other, and traveled out of Kodari toward Kathmandu.

Twenty minutes down the road, we rounded a corner. A chest-high mound of earth was blocking the dirt road, with dust swirling in the currents above. Chuck and most of the mission team were on the other side of the landslide, standing outside of their two vehicles, watching the landslide and waving in excitement from far on the other side.

Run for Your Lives

Remember how my story started? I sprinted over the landslide and was greeted with cheers and hugs. What a rush! I had to catch my breath. Then came Dilip; he was moving slower but he made it. And last, Kurt Gorton came walking over with a suitcase over his head. Several rocks bounced down the mountain, touching down several times before launching 20 feet over his head.

Kurt made it! Would anyone back home understand how crazy that was?

Feed the Hungry

We stopped in a village an hour down the road. Chuck hopped out and ran up to a box truck that was pulled over on the side of the road. We came over as they opened the back, and Chuck explained that WMA had 50-pound sacks of rice for us to pass out. The locals had heard and an excited crowd was gathering quickly. Small-statured men and women carried bags of rice, which weighed slightly less than they did, away from the truck on their heads or backs.

Where were they going to walk to? Nothing appeared habitable. What would they do when they ran out of rice? They wore smiles from ear to ear; this was like Christmas for them. Chuck explained afterward, in the SUV, that we wanted to show the love of Jesus in practical ways. *Well done, Chuck,* I thought.

I was ready to catch my flight back home the next day, with my mission accomplished.

Matthew 25:31-46 NKJV:

"When the Son of Man comes in His glory, and all the holy angels with Him, then He will sit on the throne of His glory. All the nations will be gathered before Him, and He will separate them one from another, as a shepherd divides his sheep from the goats. And He will set the sheep on His right hand, but the goats on the left. Then the King will say to those on His right hand, 'Come, you blessed of My Father, inherit the kingdom prepared for you from the foundation of the world: for I was hungry and you gave Me food; I was thirsty and you gave Me drink; I was a stranger and you took Me in; I was naked and you clothed Me; I was sick and you visited Me; I was in prison and you came to Me.'

"Then the righteous will answer Him, saying, 'Lord, when did we see You hungry and feed You, or thirsty and give You drink? When did we see You a stranger and take You in, or naked and clothe You?' Or when did we see You sick, or in prison, and come to You?' And the King will answer and say to them, 'Assuredly, I say to you, inasmuch as you did it to one of the least of these My brethren, you did it to Me.'

"Then He will also say to those on the left hand, 'Depart from Me, you cursed, into the everlasting fire prepared for the devil and his angels: for I was hungry and you gave Me no food; I was thirsty and you gave Me no drink; I was a stranger and you did not take Me in, naked and you did not clothe Me, sick and in prison and you did not visit Me.'

"Then they also will answer Him, saying, 'Lord, when did we see You hungry or thirsty or a stranger or naked or sick or in prison, and did not minister to You?' Then He will answer them, saying, 'Assuredly, I say to you, inasmuch as you did not do it to one of the least of these, you did not do it to Me.' And these will go away into everlasting punishment, but the righteous into eternal life."

First Responders

During the ride, Chuck explained that human trafficking in Nepal had gotten worse in the wake of the earthquakes. Rueben was hearing frequent reports of human traffickers taking people during the chaotic aftermath of the earthquakes. I told Chuck of a guest pastor at our Texas church, Greg Romine. Greg explained that this happens routinely around the world after disasters. He and his wife founded CalledtoRescue.org because of child sex trafficking that they stumbled upon in the Philippines. He said that yachts came to the Philippines after typhoons to carry women and children away during the chaos. Cindy Romine wrote *Called to Rescue* recounting stories of girls rescued from trafficking.

Back at the Hotel

I looked out of my sixth-floor hotel window, watching it get dark in Kathmandu. I sat at the desk and started emailing my family. It was so quiet, and I was feeling a little homesick. I was holding my cell phone in front of me, resting my elbow on the desk. The phone started rhythmically swaying back and forth. I thought I must have had a muscle spasm; I am getting older and was exhausted. But no—it was an earthquake!

I ran out the door in my pajamas and knocked on the doors of the mission members to tell them to get out of the hotel. We raced down the winding flights of stairs and out into the dark streets to be met by the stares of locals walking past. Chuck told us they were still having aftershocks and tremors, but our hotel was built with better standards than most of the buildings in the capital. After 30 minutes of awkward stares from locals walking past, we filed back into the hotel. The locals were clearly not as concerned by the aftershocks and small quakes as we were.

Following Year

World Missions Alliance had a return mission to Nepal a year later, in June 2016. They had scheduled a day of work in Kodari. The road we had run through a year before was the only way in and out of Kodari. A week before they arrived, a landslide had caused the road, and the whole mountainside, to slide into the rapids below. Plans change.

Windows of Opportunity

Windows of opportunity open for a limited time and then close. Our trip to Nepal was perfect timing. The May 2019 WMA newsletter gave evidence of the Nepali government persecution of the Church after our trip. Quoting Chuck Todd: "A few weeks ago, we received a prayer request from Pastor Reuben in Nepal. He shared with us that one of our ministry friends there along with a missionary from the United States were arrested in their hotel room. The crime they were charged with was the possession of a Bible!"

What a contrast to the open freedom we experienced in Nepal in June 2015. If the Holy Spirit prompts you to do something, don't miss out on the blessing of co-laboring with Christ!

Photos Taken in Nepal

Destruction from earthquakes in Nepal.

Another landslide in Nepal.

Clearing concrete rubble with basket.

No EMTs and nowhere to go.

Dr. Bartlett on the footbridge over rapids.

Truck damaged by avalanche boulder.

Prayer in the remote Himalayas.

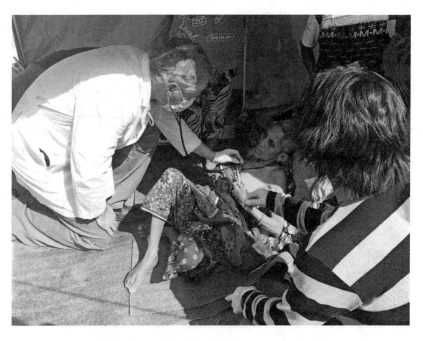

Dr. Bartlett and interpreter perform an examination.

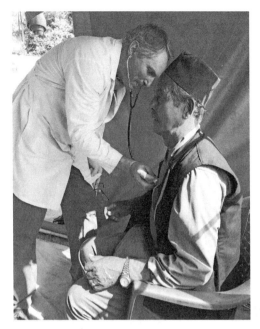

Dr. Bartlett listens to a Nepalese village elder's heart.

Dr. Bartlett and a Nepalese woman.

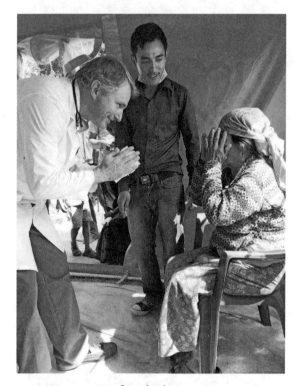

Introductions.

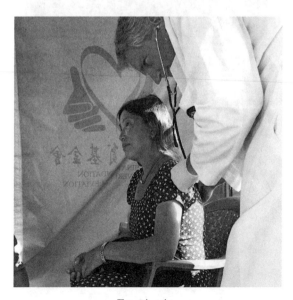

Examination.

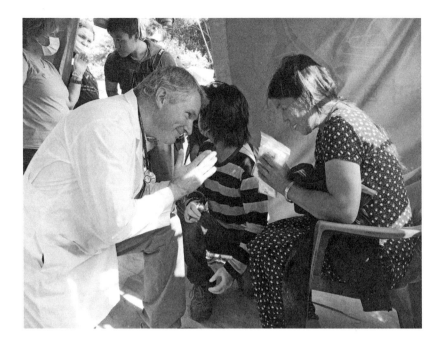

Thank yous.

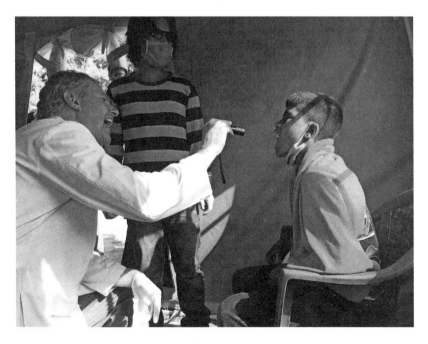

Open wide!

Tent city.

Terraced mountainsides.

A variety of modes of transportation.

Cattle in traffic.

CHAPTER 2

Doctors Defy the Dictator

February 2016
Cairo, Egypt

When I came down the stairs, I saw the narrow Cairo street through the openings in the decorative cement block wall, which functioned as windows. Movement had caught my eye even though it was just before sunrise and still dim. A dark blue police van came to an abrupt stop. Seven Egyptian troopers in black helmets and riot gear, rifles held across their chests, spilled out as the back doors flung open.

Six of them posted guard around the van. I quietly made a few team members aware of the danger and slipped into a plastic chair at one of the tables. An officer, six foot five inches tall and fit, came through the front door, boots clicking on the worn industrial tile.

With a finger on the trigger of the assault rifle across his chest, he squared up ten feet in front of me. I breathed as slowly as possible, trying not be noticed. I knew they had come for me, the American doctor. Day after day, a police informant imbedded in our group watched as I doctored patients in my white coat. They knew what I looked like—there was no blending in, no hiding.

I remembered a recent article in *The Guardian:* "Thousands of Doctors in Egypt Protest after Police are Accused of Attack of Two

Medics." The article talked about two paramilitary security force police who came into an ER and cut in line, demanding care. One of the policemen thought he needed stitches on his forehead. The doctor said, "No, it will be fine. You don't need that." The police didn't like that answer, so they beat him and the doctor next to him. They stomped on their heads with their boots. They handcuffed the two doctors, brought them down to the police station, interrogated them, beat them some more, and threatened them. They told them not to talk, but they did. As a result, thousands of doctors took to the streets in protest. Until then, if eight people gathered in public it was an unlawful gathering and often led to imprisonment, torture, and death. Thousands of Cairo doctors defied General al-Sisi with demonstrations that crippled the capital for days. Today, a second doctor demonstration was scheduled.

The trooper scanned the room from me, then to the left . . . to the right. I remained as still as possible. He never spoke. He studied other team members as they trickled into the dim room; half awake, greeting each other softly. That was the first day I had worn a well-used, blue T-shirt riddled with holes instead of a white dress shirt and tie. I was unshaven and looked like a homeless person who just crawled in off the street, not a doctor. My physical appearance matched my emotional state.

I thought, *God is going to have to handle this.* The troopers were looking for the doctor on our team to "question." Dictator General al-Sisi was crushing all opposition with torture, prison, and death. He wasn't wasting time with trials.

Six heavily armed, armored, well-rested martial law troopers versus one sick, tired, middle-aged, unarmed doctor from Texas. It didn't look like this was going to end well.

How did I get here? Let me start at the beginning . . .

Direction and Fleece

January 2016
Texas

In January of 2016, Chuck Todd told me during a phone call that he and his wife, Helen, received a prophecy. A lady at The End-Time Handmaidens and Servants Annual Convention told Helen that a doctor would be going with their mission team to Egypt. They immediately thought of me. I thanked Chuck for telling me and said I would pray about it. I had no desire to go to Egypt.

The following week, I received a call from Kristi McConnell, who works with World Missions Alliance, telling me she believed God had told her I'm going to Egypt. I thanked her and said I would pray about whether I should go to Egypt. I did not yet feel called or drawn to Egypt.

On January 8, 2016, Kristi sent me an email with the round-trip itinerary from Midland, Texas, to Egypt for $897. I called a friend, Danny Skaggs, to pray. I told Danny I did not want to leave my wife with a large credit card debt if I did not return. We prayed, asking that if the Lord wanted me to go to Egypt, may He grant me a sign. We prayed that my duplex across from the high school would sell to pay off the credit cards. It sold several weeks later. My friend Danny, who is a pharmacist, offered to donate the medicine for the free medical clinics. I still did not "feel" like going.

On January 20, 2016, Kristi sent another email. The price had gone up to $1,000 for the round-trip itinerary to Egypt.

Luke 11:2-11 NKJV:

So He said to them, "When you pray, say:

> Our Father in heaven,
> Hallowed be Your name.
> Your kingdom come.

Your will be done

On earth as *it is* in heaven.

Give us day by day our daily bread.

And forgive us our sins,

For we also forgive everyone who is indebted to us.

And do not lead us into temptation,

But deliver us from the evil one."

And He said to them, "Which of you shall have a friend, and go to him at midnight and say to him, 'Friend, lend me three loaves; for a friend of mine has come to me on his journey, and I have nothing to set before him'; and he will answer from within and say, 'Do not trouble me; the door is now shut, and my children are with me in bed; I cannot rise and give to you'? I say to you, though he will not rise and give to him because he is his friend, yet because of his persistence he will rise and give him as many as he needs.

"So I say to you, ask, and it will be given to you; seek, and you will find; knock, and it will be opened to you. For everyone who asks receives, and he who seeks finds, and to him who knocks it will be opened. If a son asks for bread from any father among you, will he give him a stone? Or if he asks for a fish, will he give him a serpent instead of a fish?"

Prayer

The cell reception was awful inside the medical clinic I worked at because it was a metal building. I would sometimes go out to the front sidewalk to make phone calls. On January 21, I was in front of the office, talking to Danny about the mission trip. Danny prayed that God would provide people to partner financially with us for missions. He had more faith than I that someone would see the need to contribute. I remained silent as Danny prayed.

Prayer Answered

After praying with Danny over the phone, I walked past the trucks parked in front of the office into the clinic building. The sun was bright, reflecting off the chrome bumpers on that hot summer day, and the truck windows were tinted. I did not notice a person sitting in one of the trucks.

Fifteen minutes later, the receptionist told me that Blane Shuffield, a friend who is a Texas Special Ranger, was there to see me. I told Blane about the martial law and human rights violations happening in Egypt under the dictator General al-Sisi, as I had learned of it through several news articles.

An article from NPR, written by Leila Fadel, described human trafficking: "Does Egypt's Law Protect 'Short-Term Brides' Or Formalize Trafficking?" (https://www.npr.org/sections/parallels/2016/02/01/463708687/does-egypts-law-protect-short-term-brides-or-formalize-trafficking)

This author interviewed several young Egyptian women who were working full time with multiple jobs for less than $100 a day, and their families were being met by "brokers" who would broker a deal so these young ladies could be sold to be Saudi businessmen's "brides" for a month or two while they were in Egypt.

A February 1, 2016 BBC article titled "Egypt cartoonist Islam Gawish briefly arrested 'over website'" described an arrest and release with no formal charge (https://www.bbc.com/news/world-middle-east-35463426).

The young Egyptian cartoonist was arrested for running a website without a license. He was actually posting satirical cartoons about martial law in Egypt on Facebook. Of course, in Egypt you don't just pay fines. You go to prison and are tortured. That was his story.

A January 26, 2016 article on Breitbart.com, "Islamic State claims responsibility for deadly Cairo attack," described the killing of nine people in a bombing attack on a busy Cairo street by ISIS (https://www.breitbart.com/national-security/2016/01/23/islamic-state-claims-responsibility-for-deadly-cairo-attack/).

A BBC article titled "Egypt steps up security for fifth anniversary of uprising" described preemptive home raids, looking for people who were planning to protest during the upcoming fifth anniversary of the toppling of President Mubarak's reign. They were expecting resistance and were moving the military into the streets (https://www.bbc.com/news/world-middle-east-35399583).

The final article I described to Blane was the February 8, 2016 BBC article titled "Giulio Regeni: Egypt rejects police role in student's death" (https://www.bbc.com/news/world-middle-east-35525871). The article talked about an Italian Ph.D. student who disappeared in Egypt's capital, Cairo, on the evening of January 25, the fifth anniversary of the uprising against former President Hosni Mubarak, when there was heavy police presence in Cairo. Regeni was a visiting scholar at the American University in Cairo, researching trade unions and labor rights in Egypt, which was a sensitive topic in recent years. When his body was found it showed inhumane signs of torture. He had left his apartment to visit a friend, but he never made it there. A week later, his naked, tortured body was found in the streets. It had all the telltale signs of how people were tortured by the Egyptian military/police.

I also described the ER incident with the doctors who were beaten, leading to a massive demonstration, defying General al-Sisi and shutting down Cairo for days.

When our conversation started winding down, Blane opened his wallet and handed me a check for $1,000. I was totally surprised. He told me God wanted him to support the medical mission trips.

He said he was in his truck waving at me while I was on the sidewalk on my phone. I hadn't seen him. The answer to our prayer had arrived at the very moment the prayer left Danny's lips. Blane explained that he was in the middle of typing a document to present to the Texas Legislature about a proposed bill concerning overweight oil rigs traveling state highways.

Suddenly, he was interrupted by a directive from the Holy Spirit: "Go to Richard now and give him a check for the Egypt mission!"

Even as Blane had the thought, *How much?* the answer was "$1,000." Blane said the Spirit insisted he drop his work, in mid-sentence of typing the document, and go! Go now.

Because Blane obeyed the Holy Spirit, I had confidence that I was to go to Egypt even though I wasn't "feeling it." That night, after I got home, I told my wife what had happened.

Preparations

I called the WMA. Kristi helped me buy my tickets. Danny shipped the donated medicine to Odessa from the new Pharmacy Unlimited headquarters in San Antonio.

Inspired Prayer

Until those doctor protests, people were arrested and severely punished when caught at public protests. The BBC reported the Egyptian dictatorship was embarrassed and seeking to decrease the publicity. The next scheduled doctor protest was February 20, in the middle of my scheduled trip to Cairo. Blane prayed that the Lord would hide the mission team from the enemy and bring us back safely. A week before the trip, I got an email from Kristi of WMA saying that Egypt required $30 and a passport picture for me to receive a visa at the Egypt airport.

Empathy

On my way home from work, I went to a local photographer to get the required passport picture for an Egyptian visa. The shop owner said he spent four years in Egypt. He often had strangers spit at his feet as he walked down sidewalks in Egypt because he wore a cross necklace. He took six photos, trying to get the perfect picture. He refused to be paid because he wanted to be a part of supporting the mission.

The Coptic Church

During a call, Chuck told me about the Coptic Church. When Saint Mark, one of the Apostles, came to Alexandria in Egypt, he spread the Gospel and it spread like wildfire. It was mainly Egyptians, not Jews or Greeks, who were living in Alexandria and had faith in Christ. Over the next 200 years, the Christian faith spread all over Egypt from Alexandria. The church became very formalized with many traditions. One thousand years ago, they were overrun by a Muslim invasion. The Muslims treated the Christians as second-class citizens. Christians were forced to convert, pay a heavy tax for not being Muslim, and live as less than, or simply be enslaved. Those who refused conversion were also forcibly branded or tattooed with a cross.

Oppressed But Not Broken

For the next 900 years, Christians were constantly oppressed in Egypt by their Muslim overlords. Despite the history of oppression, there has been evidence of great faith among the Coptic Christians throughout the centuries. Modern Coptic Christians now often choose to tattoo the inside of their right wrist with a cross as both a symbol of their faith and a symbol of their defiance. It's saying, "I am not ashamed of the Gospel of Jesus Christ (Yeshua), I am not ashamed to show that I am a Christian, and I am not afraid to die for my faith."

In February of 2015, many young Egyptian men went to the neighboring country of Libya to work and sent their paychecks to their families back home. One night, 21 Egyptian construction workers woke up to ISIS terrorists with machine guns. The terrorists checked the inside of each worker's right wrist. Each worker that had a tattoo of a cross was taken hostage.

Each of the 21 young men were later placed in orange jumpsuits and escorted by a knife-carrying terrorist, single file, onto a beach with the Mediterranean waves in the background. TV cameras and lights were in front of the captives and they were each forced to kneel as their masked captor stood behind them holding the knife to their throat.

The whole ordeal was videoed by ISIS in a slick, Hollywood-style production. Each of the captives were asked to renounce Christ. When they refused to renounce Christ, they were beheaded one by one, their blood spilling out on the beach.

One dark-skinned captive from another African nation was taken by mistake. He did not have a tattoo but was rooming with others who did. He was the last to be asked to renounce Christ or die. He saw 20 other young men beheaded, one by one. He told the ISIS captors, "Their God is my God!"

The video of the murder of the martyrs was posted on the internet by ISIS, titled "To the People of the Cross." It caused a surprising response in Egypt. The Coptic Church at large made a public proclamation that they forgave the terrorists for killing those Christians on the beach.

Helen Todd, Chuck Todd's wife, asked me if I would be willing to interview the family members of the 21 Christians martyred on the Libyan beach, while I was in Cairo. I replied that I would be honored but, knowing that ISIS, the Muslim Brotherhood, and other terrorists were in those parts, I expressed reservations about traveling five hours across the Egyptian desert toward the Ethiopian border. Chuck said the Egyptian security forces would protect us. It didn't feel right. Several weeks later, Chuck said the meeting with the martyrs' families was cancelled because the Egyptian security forces said it would be too dangerous. The Egyptian security forces recommended staying in Cairo for the entire trip, due to ISIS and related dangers.

Orphans

On Saturday morning, a week before the trip, my wife and I were enjoying coffee alone in our living room. I had the thought of calling Dwyatt Gantt of Children's Hope, an adoption agency. I told Dwyatt how I travel to many countries and, if he gave me a title that would get the attention of country leaders, I could act as an ambassador for Children's Hope. Maybe a new opportunity to help orphans could develop. Dwyatt said he had been wondering recently why he hadn't already asked me to be on the board of Children's Hope. We have the same passion for helping children and have known each other for so many years. The next day, Dwyatt sent me a text with the title of Medical Services Director. I made 500 business cards and brought some with me to Egypt.

Egypt or Bust

February 16, 2016

My wife and son gave me a ride to Midland International Airport. The airline's extra baggage charge on my last trip was expensive. I asked the United Airline attendant who was checking my baggage if there was a discount for humanitarian aid. She said she recognized me from being on TV and knew I was going on a medical mission. She thought she could help. She called her boss and got both of my bags checked for free all the way to Egypt. She had a fellow zip-tie the bags and she placed several extra stickers on them so no one would inspect the bags. She gave my wife and son a pass to go through the security point so they could eat lunch with me at the airport restaurant before I flew out. What a pleasant beginning to the mission!

Trouble Begins

I flew to Houston. During my layover in Houston, I started having chills and body aches. Danny Skaggs prayed with me on the phone. I considered aborting the mission and going back home. I refused to be so easily defeated and decided to board the plane for Frankfurt. I got sicker with fever, sweating, and nausea. My abdomen became so distended that I was uncomfortable bending my hips to sit in the airplane seat.

Fervent Prayers

Despite praying, throughout the flight I continued to feel worse. I was praying for direction as to whether or not I should return home from Frankfurt and abort the trip. Surely there is a reason, maybe spiritual, that I am in this situation. What can I do? I recalled all the things that could hinder my prayers. A lack of forgiveness can hinder prayer. I racked my brain for anyone who had done me wrong that I may have forgotten to forgive. I forgave everyone to make sure I had nothing hindering my prayers. At 40,000 feet in the airplane toilet, I repeatedly forgave them and prayed blessings on them. I earnestly tried to cooperate with all that I understood of Biblical instructions about prayer. I even prayed for the peace of Jerusalem. I returned to my seat, cramped between two obese men.

After seven hours of misery in flight, I asked the flight attendant for water. I took three sips of water because my mouth was dry. Three sips was too many. I hurried to the restroom past sleeping passengers. On my knees in the cramped restroom, bouncing around due to turbulence, I braced my knees and elbows against the walls. I vomited and heaved. Weak and shaky, I opened the door and walked to my seat past the awakened and disgusted. I was demoralized and emotionally exhausted. I had prayed and did all I could. Things were going the wrong direction fast. I would abort the mission and return home.

Made It to Germany

February 17, 2016
Frankfurt, Germany

When I got to the Frankfurt airport, I planned to give the team the baggage claim tickets for my suitcases of medicine so they could make a new plan, possibly with a local Christian doctor.

THE DOCTOR'S TRAVEL JOURNAL

Then, I saw the familiar face I was looking for. My friend, Morgan McCasland is a tall, middle-aged man sporting a moustache. He was dressed casually and walked toward me out of the crowd.

He smiled as he extended his hand in greeting. "How was your flight, Richard?"

"I'm not feeling well, Morgan. I'm going to head back home. I am really sick." I handed Morgan the checked baggage claim tickets for the medical supplies and told him he and the team would have to come up with a last-minute plan without me. Chuck Todd joined us shortly after, and I explained again that I was very ill and was going to head back to the United States. Morgan and Chuck prayed with me. Chuck suggested that I try a little Sprite. I reasoned that I had nothing to lose so I bought a Sprite.

Thirty minutes later, I had kept half a bottle of Sprite down. Before that, I hadn't eaten for 24 hours and hadn't kept liquids down. I decided to press on to Cairo. I drank a coffee and a Sprite on the flight from Frankfurt to Cairo. I skipped the meal. I had missed three in-flight meals and, until then, the smell of food had caused nausea.

First Impressions of Cairo

We landed at the Cairo airport at 2:00 am. After I picked up my two huge suitcases, everyone was funneled past a luggage X-ray machine. The guard scanned the lady's bag in front of me. I started to roll my suspiciously large suitcases to the machine. The guard made eye contact and waved me out of the line. I looked, and smelled, like I'd been sick and traveling for 24 hours. The airport radiated third world with its hint of sewer gas and security officers with assault rifles. On the curb, local men grabbed for our bags as we rolled out of the airport into the fresh night air. They were gesturing and speaking loudly in Arabic; it was clear that they were competing, trying to speak over each other. I watched over the older women of our team to make sure they made it through the flock of noisy, grabby men. We loaded into two white vans in the parking lot. Green rope lights wrapped around tall palm trees reminded me that I was not in West Texas anymore.

Two men watched us from their car, parked in the dark lot. I was exhausted and weak, but I kept an eye on them. Meanwhile, our luggage was being stacked high on the roof. It seemed to take a long time to rope the luggage down. The vans took off and drove past dreary, old, gray, urban Cairo. We passed occasional security posts in the shadowy periphery. We exited a four-lane highway and wound through streets that narrowed to one lane between unlit buildings.

Christian Hotel

When we arrived at the "Christian" hotel, we met the host pastor, Romani, and his wife, Lilian.

Lilian was the conversationalist of the duo. Lilian's kind face was in a perpetual smile under big brown eyes. Romani had a short haircut, a lean, fit frame, and a no-nonsense expression. The colorful fashion attire of his wife, who was glamorized with makeup and fashion jewelry, balanced the austere Romani. She gave us a brief summary of the week's agenda. She even planned for us to visit an orphanage! I told her and Chuck about my conversation with Dwyatt and gave them some of my newly printed Adoption Agency business cards. Lilian also explained that the police would be traveling with us to keep an eye on us, not to protect us. We were told to choose our words and actions very carefully, so the security wouldn't react adversely.

Flurry of Upsetting Reports

Chuck got me a private room so I could recover. Chuck and his roommate, Mike, prayed for me in the dark hall between our rooms. Mike was a tall, blond, former high school basketball star attending college. He was skilled at videography and had accumulated video and camera equipment. He joined the team to document events of the mission. While we were praying, Mike received a text and read it to Chuck and me. Some young ladies associated with the WMA had texted Mike that someone had just broke into their house. They could hear the intruders downstairs in their dark apartment. We prayed right then for the women. I, almost simultaneously, had a picture text with a message light up my phone: a tenant of the duplex I own near my home said the empty unit next to his was broken into. The picture was the door ajar with a broken doorframe. I texted a police officer friend back home, who said he would take care of it. Mike got a text that the girls heard the intruders make a clamor as they escaped, when the police knocked on the ladies' front door.

In My Hotel Room

I called my wife and learned that my family was dealing with a flurry of problems at home. Sink faucets wouldn't turn off at my house. The car's trunk latch wouldn't work so the trunk wouldn't open. A skunk sprayed my dog.

I took some medicine and tried to catch some sleep. I had Christian music playing on my iPod all night. Outside my window, the noises were plentiful; dogs barking, random screams, moaning, and gunshots interrupted the night. The Muslim droning of prayers was loud in the predawn hours. I found out later that a mosque was across the street, in what looked like a six-story block building. No minaret was present, which masked the regular activities from me for several days. That explained the volume of the droning prayers over loudspeakers.

Sleep was interrupted and fitful. Anxiety kept coming on, which triggered me to pray. At 4:00 a.m., I had the new symptom of vertigo. I still had lightheadedness, and some abdominal pains and bloating, but no nausea. It was clear that my symptoms were not resolving. I decided I would get a ticket in the morning to return to the U.S.

February 18, 2016
Cairo

The sun came up and I felt less miserable. I didn't feel well but decided to do the clinic. We saw 52 patients in our first free medical clinic at a church. When I started to tell the Good News, the translator interrupted and told me they were all Christian. I was too weak to argue, as I was the most acutely ill person at the clinic. I anointed and prayed for several people, but saw no visible results. In the van, I couldn't tell who was the local pastor or who was the police watching us, because everyone was dressed the same.

Following the fruitful pattern of the medical mission to Nepal, patients were triaged and had their vital signs and medical history written down on index cards. The cards were handed to the patients. The patients would then go to a room to have a prayer team intercede for them. Finally, they would be seen by me and the Canadian ICU nurse, Erroll Koshman, for medical care. A hired translator also accompanied us. That day's translator kept insisting that everyone who came for care was a Christian. She kept discouraging me from telling the Gospel, insistent that they were already Christian. No miracles or salvations happened in my exam room. Lunch was chicken sandwiches from a restaurant. Half a sandwich and I was getting abdominal pain and bloating. I was still weak and light-headed.

A church leader asked me to come to his home and pray for his mother on dialysis. Erroll and I walked down the dark streets to his apartment. He offered Turkish coffee, which I drank, hoping my guts would start working. We went back to the church for an evening service. During Chuck's sermon, I had to find the restroom. The abdominal pain decreased. At the end of the service, team members placed their hands on the heads of the sick and prayed for them. The policeman who was monitoring us placed Chuck's hand on his head and motioned for Chuck to pray for him.

A Long Night

I took some medicine and went to bed exhausted. I had my iPod filling the room with Christian music. A Muslim prayer went over the loudspeakers several times, competing with the barking, yelling, and gunshots scattered throughout the night. Anxiety without a specific trigger caused me to pray throughout the night, in tongues and Scriptures.

I had fitful sleep once again. Every time I started to relax and go unconscious I woke because I felt a pressure on my abdomen and my
abdominal pain increased. It decreased as I became more alert. I also
woke up four times to diarrhea. At first, I was glad that the bloating
was less, but then I started feeling weaker despite drinking a bottle of
water. I woke Chuck for Imodium and prayer. Chuck said he sometimes
listened to the Bible on his phone to go to sleep. I said I sometimes did
that as well but my phone couldn't google the Bible app that I normally
used. Biblegateway.com was apparently blocked in Egypt.

I texted Tim Storey, a friend who leads the Hollywood Bible Study:
"Please intercede for me in Egypt: Sick. Thanks, Richard. Let me know
if you have wisdom for me, don't want to upset my wife." And Tim
texted back: "I'm praying my friend, right now! Love you!! Psalm 23."

I was on my knees, sincerely pressing for the Lord. I repeatedly
prayed out loud Psalm 23 with conviction to combat the terror that
was trying to unravel me. I put emphasis on a different word each time
I prayed Psalm 23 out loud to the Lord. The room was spinning from
vertigo, I had chills, and I was clammy and weak.

Jeremiah

I again woke Chuck and borrowed his phone to listen to the Bible.
Chuck's phone would only play the book of Jeremiah. Jeremiah is
not the most encouraging and calming book in the Bible. I listened
to God tell about the extreme stubbornness and insolence of the
Jewish people, and the terrible doom coming their way. I hung onto
the slightest positive words and repeatedly repented of any possible
offenses toward God. My heart pounded. I was weak, lightheaded,
off-balance, and had waves of abdominal pain. My ears were ringing. My legs were swelling, and I was short of breath. My skin was
clammy. I took a shower but it didn't make me feel any better. Using
my iPhone, I checked flights out of Egypt and back to Texas. My
symptoms were worsening instead of resolving. I didn't have confi-

dence that I would be well received as an American missionary at a
Cairo ER with Muslim doctors.

February 19, 2016
Cairo

In the Friday morning meeting, Chuck suggested we take the day off.
He said he would rather lose a day than the whole trip. Chuck, Paulie,
and James anointed me and prayed for God to heal me. I was still light-
headed and weak with vertigo. I insisted on going with the team and
providing care at the clinic. In whispers, I was told the stranger in the
passenger seat of the van was a police plant keeping an eye on us. I
saw only 18 patients because Friday is the main Islamic worship day
in Egypt. Again, every time I started to share the Good News with a
patient, the translator argued that they were already Christians, and
resisted translating. I was too weak to argue. I was definitely the sickest
person in the clinic that day. No salvations or miracles happened during
that clinic. I took a Levaquin and rested in my room during the evening.
I skipped the evening service. I felt less dizzy, but still weak. I joined
everyone in the dining hall for a 10 p.m. dinner. We had spicy chicken
crepes, pimento cream cheese pastry, and cornbread with chocolate
muffin in the middle. I was hungry and ate the whole meal.

I went to bed, but had trouble falling asleep despite my exhaustion.
Muslim prayer on loudspeakers, dogs barking, and plenty of yelling
made for another fitful night. The anxiety kept coming. I read Psalm 23
out loud, repeatedly, and with conviction. I called home and my wife
answered. I hung on every syllable, wanting to tell her how bad I felt,
but restraining myself so she wouldn't worry. She told me our oldest
son, who was working as a substitute high school teacher, came back
from break to find a folded note on his desk. In the empty room, he
flipped it over to see who it was from. No clues who left it. Opening the
note, he found it was filled with nonsense and death curses against his

family. He tore it up and prayed to rebuke the curses, in Jesus' name. That has never happened before or since with my family.

February 20, 2016
Cairo

Early on Saturday, I woke in the dark with a hot sensation in my lower belly; not tender, not medical, but very concerning. I saw I had missed Eva Dooley's call an hour before, so I returned her call. Eva is an experienced missionary. She said she had been thinking of us, so she called my wife and they prayed for me. Eva and her husband, Bill, prayed with me for my health. She said my illness was a demonic attack, and not the result of a medical illness. She called it a "spirit of infirmity," for lack of better words. She said she had a vision of another demonic presence harassing me like a wasp flying around. Eva asked if Chuck had anointed me, since he was the authority of the team. I told her yes. She then asked me to call Mark Bristow, a missionary and mutual friend of ours.

Prayer With Mark

Mark answered my call. He said he and Larry Maruffo had just passed my house in Texas on the highway and prayed for me, not knowing I was in Egypt at that very moment. He said he had been captivated with Egypt for the last four days. He had watched every YouTube documentary about Egypt he could find. He had been frequently praying for Egypt. He even had a dream that he was in a chamber of the pyramids, taking authority over the false gods of Egypt. Mark and I prayed. During prayer, he said there are powerful, ancient, spiritual forces abroad, and it is common to have difficulty sleeping while in these countries. He felt that God was about to do a mighty work in Egypt. He said the demonic spiritual forces in Egypt are on the same level as in Iraq.

Mark said the evil Egyptian spirits had thrown down their staves for false signs and miracles against me, but I will throw down my staff, the symbol of my authority in Christ, and have the victory. Mark reminded me of the Scripture Ephesians 6:12 (TLB):

For we are not fighting against people made of flesh and blood, but against persons without bodies—the evil rulers of the unseen world, those mighty satanic beings and great evil princes of darkness who rule this world; and against huge numbers of wicked spirits in the spirit world.

While praying with Mark, he said the devil is a liar. The Holy Spirit reminded me of the plague against the firstborn sons that occurred in Egypt. I am a firstborn son. I understood that Satan was trying to wrongly apply that curse to me. Satan is a liar, and a trespasser, that only comes to kill, steal, and destroy. Mark told me to pray with his dear friends, Sharon and Philip Buss, who were on the mission team. He said there was no stronger prayer team than that married couple.

Prayer With Philip and Sharon

It was 6:30 a.m. and there was not yet a peep in the hotel. I crept down the dark hallway and knocked on Philip and Sharon's hotel door. Philip said they were praying and they invited me in. They held my arms up like Aaron and Hur did for Moses, as a show of support for me in my spiritual battle. Philip prayed the curses be turned into blessings and a harvest.

Philip said we were seated in heavenly places with Jesus Christ, above attacks from the enemy. God laughs at the enemy's plans, and we should imitate God, and laugh at the enemy plans as well. Philip said we should laugh at the attack and then started to laugh on purpose. Sharon and I followed suit. It felt awkward. I was sick and did not feel like laughing. I did it anyway. I know that I'm supposed to go with what I believe instead of what I feel. We praised the Lord.

Sharon said, "The Lord says we should do communion daily, and you should tell your family to do the same." Sharon advised me to anoint the walls, doors, and windows of my hotel room, and pray for the room to be clear of every ungodly presence.

Psalm 31:20 TLB:

> Hide your loved ones in the shelter of your presence, safe beneath your hand, safe from all conspiring men.

They Have Come for Me

After I prayed with Philip and Sharon, I headed down the dark hall on my way to the dining room, dressed in my ragged, faded T-shirt, and sat down at a table after notifying the team of the arrival of the van full of riot troops. This was the day Cairo physicians had a second major demonstration scheduled in response to the police brutality against ER doctors that had happened several weeks before.

Troopers stood with rifles ready outside. The tall officer in black riot gear with rifle ready stood facing me in the quiet dining room. Fifteen long minutes passed as he silently studied each person in the room.

At the same time in West Texas, Texas Special Ranger Blane Shuffield sat up in his dark bedroom from a sound sleep. He was immediately awake and alert. Shuffield clearly heard the Holy Spirit say, "Pray now for Richard!" He had strong irresistible urges to pray in the Spirit punctuated by Scriptures of protection. He prayed repeatedly that his brother in Christ would be hidden from the enemy.

The Egyptian trooper turned and walked out the front door. He waved the other troopers back into the van. They left as quickly as they had appeared. I was spared certain torture and prison.

Communion Is the Key

Just like every day of this mission, the abdominal pain and associated symptoms, though present, decreased in the morning. Chuck explained the itinerary for the day in the after-breakfast meeting. After two worship songs and prayer, we had communion. Communion consisted of pieces of local flatbread dipped in a coffee cup of mango juice as the cup was passed around. Upon receiving the elements of communion, all symptoms immediately stopped! Peace was tangible. I told the team

I sensed a shift in the atmosphere. We should expect God to do mighty things in the clinic. Other team members said they sensed the change as well.

Miracles During Clinic

We rode in a van to the church for clinic. A policeman in plain clothes was with us, as usual, in the front passenger seat of the van. On that day, most of the patients were not church members. All were poor, and many identified as Coptic Christians. Due to the previous translator's frequent interruptions during prayer and care, and refusal to translate exactly what I was saying, I asked for a new translator. Pastor Romani's wife, Lilian, served as translator and relayed everything I said without opposition.

We worked through lunch, neither hungry nor aware of time. There were miracles and salvations. I experienced what Jesus meant in John 4:32-34 (NIV):

But he said to them, "I have food to eat that you know nothing about."

Then his disciples said to each other, "Could someone have brought him food?"

"My food," said Jesus, "is to do the will of him who sent me and to finish his work."

I had no weakness or hunger. Out of concern, Pastor Romani brought us Pepsi, Titis (an Egyptian cupcake), and Moro candy bars at 3 p.m.

The first patients were a woman with two small children. I asked what symptoms she was having and how we could help. She said she and the children had no health problems. She said she did not know why she was at the church for a medical clinic. She had heard of the scheduled clinic months before and knew she was supposed to come. They traveled from a small village, three hours away, to the clinic. With Lilian translating, I told the mother and kids the Best News in the World. I asked if they had heard the Gospel of Jesus before. They had not. I asked if they would like to accept the gift of life with God that Jesus had purchased for them. They said yes. Tears were flowing down the mother's face as she and her children prayed in unison. Her joy was obvious after the prayer. She asked us to pray for her husband, for his salvation, and for financial help.

Many Healed Through Prayer

Many were healed—shoulders, knees, backs, headaches, wrists. I was surprised by how many people had cross tattoos on their wrists but had not heard the Gospel or prayed for salvation. It made me think of 18-year-old boys signing up for the U.S. military, not really understanding the details of foreign policies they would be risking death to enforce.

Wrist Pain

An older woman came for help because of severe pain in her right wrist for the past five months. She said she could not turn her right wrist to lock the door when she left home. She'd had an Egyptian doctor do a cortisone injection in her wrist, but it gave no relief. She said the pain was a 10 on a scale of 1 to 10. The right wrist was swollen, and twice the diameter of the left wrist. We anointed her with oil and prayed for her. After prayer, smiling, she was able to twist her wrist around in the full range of motion. She said she was pain-free for the first time in months. Her daughter sat quietly next to her mother throughout the visit. Seeing her mother pain-free after prayer left her wide-eyed and nervous. The daughter did not want prayer and moved away from us, scared.

Arm Pain

The third person of that day's clinic was an old woman with a compression sleeve on her left arm. She said her pain level had been a 10 for the past six years. She'd had breast cancer surgery and, as a result, ended up with lymphedema of the arm. She wore a compression sleeve in an attempt to decrease the swelling. The back of her hand was swollen like a balloon from the compression sleeve constricting the venous and lymphatic flow. Erroll, the ICU nurse helping me, and I anointed her and prayed. She told the translator that the pain was gone! I asked her to do something she couldn't do before due to the pain. She quickly started moving her fingers and arms. She had not lifted the left arm for years, so the shoulder deltoid muscles were weak and atrophied. She grabbed her left wrist to repeatedly raise both arms up. By faith, she used her right hand to lift the left above her head and let go. It would fall, and she would repeat. She was smiling and so excited. Her sister with knee pain was also healed.

Knee Pain

An older lady with joint pain said it especially hurt to climb stairs. She said her pain had been a 10 on a severity scale of 1 to 10 for years. We anointed and prayed for her. During prayer, the thought came to me to have her walk the stairs at the church. I asked Erroll to walk down and up the stairs with her. She was smiling for the first time as she returned. She said the pain was much less. Erroll took her a second time on the stairs. Erroll couldn't keep up with her as she returned to say the pain was gone! I asked her to jump up and down three times. She looked at me like I was crazy. Then she surprised me by jumping. She was laughing, and everyone in the church started praising the Lord. The clinic ended with rolls of laughter and Hallelujahs.

Victory Feast

We returned to a victory meal of fried beef, rice pilaf with raisins, green beans, and coffee. I called Mark to tell the great report of our day at the clinic. He said he would call Eva to let her know about the great day. Errol and I told our end of the dining table about our past trip to Kurdistan. We all cried as I told of the mother who forgave ISIS for raping and murdering her daughter. Everyone left after dinner except

James, Randy, Paulie, and me. Paulie Lamendola said he believed we should give thanks for the day's blessings. We knelt in the dining hall and prayed.

Call Home

I called my wife from my room. I told her about the great day we'd had. I asked her to start having family communion together. I told her that, physically, I felt better after communion. She told me my second oldest son went to Dallas to help my brother work on his cabin. Two former classmates from our hometown now live in Dallas. They picked him up and stayed out until 1:30 a.m. My wife and my brother were worried about him but, thankfully, my son returned home safe.

She went on to tell me my 7-year-old son's 1-year-old dog, Raider, started losing weight and looking sick. She made an appointment for Raider to see the veterinarian. She said that, when she prayed, she heard it would be a difficult trip but I would be okay.

Sleepy and peaceful, I laid down but couldn't sleep. I turned the light back on and anointed the walls, doors, and windows. I commanded the unclean spirits to leave and declared that none were allowed to come into my room. That was another instruction from the morning prayer time with the Buss couple.

February 21, 2016
Cairo

After my first night of restful sleep, I woke at 4:53 a.m. on Sunday. I decided to write down what had happened on this trip thus far. Suddenly, I felt a sensation of energy going up and down my spine. I had felt that sensation decades prior when I was baptized with the Holy Spirit. I was singing along with my iPod to Amazing Grace at the same time. I turned the iPod off and a new song I hadn't heard before came out of my mouth. The words were, "The Great I Am, mighty to save." Tears fell down my cheeks, which is rare. I realized there was a blessed silence;

the dogs were quiet, and there was no yelling, no gunshots, and no anxiety throughout the night. I felt healthy and peaceful.

I went down to breakfast and found that three team members had suffered fitful nights, just as I had previously. They were experiencing the same anxiety, cough, abdominal pains, and feeling of overwhelm that I had dealt with. One said she was considering going back home. The nurse named Traci had a nightmare that her mother had a stroke. She was convinced that bad news was coming. She was thinking about going home to help her mother. She kept asking Chuck if he had any messages about her mother from the WMA office back in the States. Chuck said no. After 20 years of doing mission trips, he has learned not to call home during the trips to avoid distractions. The devil will try to distract us by any means possible. Our mission members preached at the Sunday services we attended.

February 22, 2016
Cairo

Monday, I woke up with chills. Because the Lord deserved it, and out of anger for the new attack, I praised the Lord. I laughed on purpose at the attack and then prayed. The sensation of power flowing up and down my spine, which occurred at my baptism in the Holy Spirit, occurred again as I praised the Lord. My chills stopped, without meds or time! I felt strong and healthy and got ready for the day. While waiting for the van to pick us up, Philip Buss told us about spiritual battles on prior mission trips. One of his mission teams was passing out Gospel tracts while they climbed steep stairs up to a Tibetan monastery. A monk grabbed a tract out of a missionary's hand and ran into a room full of monks. Loud chatting followed. Later, the same monk jumped out at the same team member, kicked his ankle, and fled. The kicked team member immediately developed severe symptoms and was debilitated for the rest of the trip. Philip shared other examples of spiritual attacks on health from his missions in Tibet and to South Dakota Native Americans.

Clinic in the Lobby

The women on our team did a women's conference at one of the Egyptian churches. While waiting for them to rejoin us for a medical clinic, I tried talking to the receptionist at the lobby desk. The conversation went nowhere, due to the language barrier, so I went on about my business. Hours later, as we were preparing to leave, I was standing in the lobby. The same receptionist appeared behind me.

She presented me with her X-rays, labs, and doctor's notes, all in Arabic. I perceived from the X-rays that she had knee and ankle pain. I reviewed the records but, of course, could not read Arabic. It was clear by the dates on the X-rays that she had been suffering for about six months. Paulie and I prayed and anointed her. I asked Paulie to walk her around the dining hall. When she returned she was smiling and said the pain was gone. I asked her to do something she couldn't do before. She bent her knees, hopped on one foot, and said the pain was gone.

After the morning women's conference, Lilian, our translator, rejoined our team. She said her husband, Pastor Romani, was called by the police at 4 a.m. and grilled about who our team really was. They accused us of not really being tourists. He started to explain about the medical clinics. They said whatever we did in the church was a part of our religion. The police began threatening and yelling at Romani. He yelled back at the police and hung up.

Veiled Spiritual Attack

On the way to the clinic, we stopped at Burger King. I asked if the team could stay in the van so we would not draw unnecessary attention. Pastor Romani went in to get our food. I cracked my window, hoping for a breeze because we were already cooking in the sweltering heat. An older woman in gray local clothes on the sidewalk approached with a crazy look in her eyes. She came to my window, repeatedly saying, "I love you," in a singsong voice, while wagging a finger at us. I held my hand up in the international sign for stop and she touched the middle of my palm with her finger. What just happened? In my hand and forearm, I felt a sensation similar to when you hit your ulnar nerve (funny bone) in the elbow. The woman blended into the crowd on the sidewalk. I closed the window and started praying in tongues. I asked Sharon to pray over my hand. Lenora had a written prayer against witchcraft that she gave to Sharon, who led us in a corporate prayer. The sensation went away. Philip had just told me about the Tibetan monk encounter.

Open Heavens

We arrived at the church where our clinic would be that day. It was a new location on the eighth floor. I gave strategies for each team member, including anointing walls, doors, and windows with oil while praying prior to starting the clinic. I had James be the doorman in front of my exam room so I would not be interrupted while with patients.

We returned to the church where we held our last clinic. We had to leave without seeing everyone. Everyone who had not heard the Good News for the first time chose to pray for salvation and accepted the Lord. Everyone that had a physical problem was healed. A local Christian woman, who was helping translate for the nurses, developed severe abdominal pain during the clinic. During prayer and anointing, immediately, the woman reported that she became pain-free. The hired van driver decided to be seen as a patient and received prayer. I told him the Good News and he prayed to accept the Lord. He was our last patient. I sensed an open Heaven with immediate healings, answered prayers, and salvations.

February 23, 2016
Cairo

The next day, a new plain-clothes police officer rode with us everywhere. The Cairo museum is in front of Freedom Square, also called Martyrs Square or Tahrir Square. It was the large open area that was on CNN during the Arab Spring. Freedom Square was ground zero for the protests that led to the overthrow of Mubarak. As we unloaded from our van, we saw there were five armored vehicles with large caliber machine guns pointed at us. They were parked on the perimeter of the square. The mummies, statues, and other artifacts that were found in pyramids, and other sites, are in the museum. There was a tangible evil presence in some of the rooms of the museum. We ate lunch at a restaurant on Mokattum, a town built on top of the Mountain that Moved.

Mark 11:22-26 NIV:

"Have faith in God," Jesus answered. "Truly I tell you, if anyone says to this mountain, 'Go, throw yourself into the sea,' and does not doubt in their heart but believes that what they say will happen, it will be done for them. Therefore I tell you, whatever you ask for in prayer, believe that you have received it, and it will be yours. And when you stand praying, if you hold anything against anyone, forgive them, so that your Father in heaven may forgive you your sins."

Mountain Moving Faith

Chuck told us about Mokattam. The mountain is the site of an ancient miracle of the Lord. Around the year 975 A.D., a major event happened in Egypt. The nation of Egypt had already been overrun by the Muslim invasion (jihad). The Muslim leader would have religious leaders debate in his presence. He would allow them to state their cases as long as they were respectful. In one such debate, the leader of the Christians of Egypt, named Pope Abraham, was debating with a Jewish leader. Pope Abraham of the Coptic Christian church was getting the upper hand in the debate.

The Jewish leader decided he would press the Coptic Pope. He quoted Jesus from the Gospel in Mathew 17:20: "If you have faith as a mustard seed, you will say to this mountain, 'Move from here to there,' and then it will move, and nothing will be impossible for you." (Matthew 17:20 NKJV)

The Muslim leader asked the Coptic Pope if that was true. Abraham said that yes, it truly does say that. The Muslim leader pointed to a nearby mountain and told him to move the mountain. The Coptic Pope asked for several days to fast and pray. The Muslim dictator granted the time and warned that he would slaughter Christians if the mountain was not moved. Pope Abraham asked all Christians to fast and pray. Abraham was told, during prayer, that the Lord would not move the mountain in response to his prayers. Instead, He would move it when a poor man named Simon prayed. The Pope was told to look for a poor man carrying water jars named Simon the tanner. He was told where to find Simon. When Abraham found him, he saw that Simon only had one eye.

Take God at His Word

When Simon the tanner was a young man, he took Jesus' words literally when He said,

"If your right eye causes you to sin, pluck it out and cast it from you; for it is more profitable for you that one of your members perish, than for your whole body to be cast into hell." (Matthew 5:29-30 NKJV)

When he was young, Simon the tanner was making shoes for a beautiful young lady and had lustful thoughts. In order to quell his lustful thoughts, he plucked out his eye. Now Abraham was asking Simon to move a mountain and Simon said he felt he was not worthy; he was a poor, unimportant tanner with one eye and Abraham must have the wrong man. Abraham told him they were in a desperate situation. Simon the tanner prayed, and the mountain moved. The Muslim leader became a Christian.

The story of the mountain that moved has been recorded in history and geology books of Egypt for generations. In 1991, the skeleton of Simon the tanner was found buried in a shallow grave, underneath an ancient church that had paintings on the walls depicting the miracle of the mountain that moved. When the Muslim Brotherhood re-gained control of Egypt after the Arab Spring, the story of Simon the tanner and the mountain that moved was stricken from the records. All Muslims and Christians of Egypt had been taught for over 1,000 years that the mountain moving was a literal fact. It has been taught that the mountain was moved from Tahrir Square, AKA Freedom Square or Martyrs Square, to present-day Mokattam.

Hushed Prayers on the Mountain God Moved

We went out to the edge of the mountain so we could take pictures of Cairo and Giza, laid out below us. The police escort watched the team. We prayed quietly for the people of Egypt whenever he would walk out of earshot. The grey haze of air pollution covered most of the city. After lunch on top of Mokattum, we drove through Trash City, which is in the city dump.

Trash City

One of the consequences of the Muslim invasion 1,000 years ago was that the Christians of Egypt were treated as second-class citizens and slaves. Cairo and Giza are a metroplex of over 20 million people and generate a great deal of trash.

An enormous trash dump is located outside of Cairo. The Christians were forced by the Muslim invaders to live in the trash. Over time, a city was built in the midst of, and out of, that trash dump. Approximately 15,000 people live there now. The city has restaurants, houses, church-es, and so forth. Small pickup trucks, with mounds of trash to recycle heaped three times the height of the truck, moved slowly through the streets. Kids played in the streets, oblivious to the stench and sights of the city dump. Raw legs of lamb, goat, and beef hung on hooks in the open air of first-floor butcher shops, amidst the trash and putrid stench. The downtown buildings are very tall, with narrow winding roads, all surrounded by mounds of trash. The stench is thick and nauseating.

Generations of Christians have been raised in that atmosphere. The locals call it Zabbeleen Village.

Cave Church

We rode to the base of the Mountain that Moved, to the Cave Church. The formal name of the church is the Virgin Mary and Saint Simon the Tanner Cathedral, and the Saint Simon the Tanner Monastery. When National celebrations would use fireworks or when there would be artillery during times of war, the people of the trash city would use dynamite to expand the church. They would synchronize their explosions with the fireworks, or with the artillery booming elsewhere, and now a very large Christian church exists in the cave with an amphitheater connected to it.

News From Home

That evening, I spoke to my wife. She told me our third son was driving home from work and saw two German Shepherds in the street. He has a German Shepard and many times has had to round her up when she gets out of our yard. He loves that dog and would not want her to get hit by a car. Naturally, he pulled over and approached the dogs to see if they had tags so he could get them home safely. The dogs saw him walking and attacked, biting his ankles and feet as he sprinted back to the truck. His legs were in excruciating pain. He was surprised to see that his work boots protected him from having broken skin!

February 24, 2016
Cairo

On Wednesday, we went to a clinic at a local kindergarten until 1:30 p.m. Then, at 2:30 p.m., we went to do a clinic at a "Christian" orphanage. The orphans who heard the Good News for the first time during the clinic chose to pray and ask Jesus into their hearts. Though it was a "Christian" orphanage, three teachers who were treated in the clinic prayed to accept Jesus as Savior and Lord. I spoke a personal prophecy to a 26-year-old teacher. While I was at the orphanage, I called Dwyatt Gantt, the director of Children's Hope Adoption Agency in the U.S. He spoke to the orphanage director on my phone. The orphanage director's son translated for them.

February 25, 2016
Cairo

The next day, I woke up to a text that the nurse practitioner would not be able to cover my clinic back in West Texas. My dad said he would cover my clinic. I found out later he didn't stay, and the clinic manager had flown in from Dallas unannounced to find no doctor. She said she would not bill the company for that day. I decided I would not bill the management company and trusted that was the end of the matter.

After breakfast, we had the usual prayer meeting. During the meeting, Sharon explained that different countries have curses on their lands due to murders, sexual sins, witchcraft, and idolatry. She said that, in other countries she had been to on mission trips, they would do a ceremony to redeem the land. Jesus (Yeshua) paid the price for all redemption once and for all. However, until someone intercedes for a land, it is still under the curse. So we went outside of the hotel onto a small patch of dirt.

Redeeming the Land

Sharon gathered some of the team on the sidewalk outside of the "Christian hotel." She led a prayer ritual to redeem and heal the land of Egypt. It was across the street from a mosque. We found out later it is very dangerous to have public prayer outside of a church in Egypt, let alone across the street from a mosque, due to Sharia law. We loaded into vans to tour the pyramids of Giza. I was feeling stronger and excited about going home. I rode a camel for a victory lap around all three of the pyramids.

My young son's dog, Raider, had surgery that revealed a large, mesenteric tumor blocking nutrient absorption. He died. The veterinarian did an autopsy and found that Raider had cancer from head to toe. I believed the symptoms I was having were a result of a curse. When I did the communion, my symptoms immediately resolved. Unfortunately, Raider became ill and died.

February 26, 2016
Cairo

It was Friday and the end of the trip at last. We were sitting in the van, parked at the curb. Luggage was being loaded on top of the van. We were almost ready to go to the airport. I saw Pastor Mattie, a black lady pastor from New York. We did not get to visit much during the trip. She told me how God saved her son's life after being hit by a car in front her home. I asked her to pray a blessing on me.

The prayer turned to prophecy: "You have entered a new level. You knew you could not count on your own strength, and you trusted Me. You will see many more miracles. Many new nations for you. You will speak to organs, kidneys, and livers and they will line up with the Word. Ask what you want now, and it will be granted."

At that moment, I prayed for healing for my wife and children, a new eye for my second-oldest son, and future Godly spouses for my children.

As I was going through the security checkpoint at the Cairo airport, I got separated from the group. An agent, the Egyptian equivalent of the TSA, pressed me for a bribe. I gave him 25 EL, which is about the price of a coffee. I had some swelling in my legs on the flight back, which was unusual before this trip.

More Prophecy

Texas

The Sunday after I got back home to Texas, I gave a report of my trip to Parker Heights Church. Blane Shuffield came to hear the report. I asked Mark Bristow to pray for my family at the close of the service. Mark started to pray. Without knowing about my previous prophecy from Pastor Mattie, his prayer turned into a similar prophecy: "You have entered a new level. I am pleased. Many new countries for you to go to. You will hear a voice behind you saying this is the way, turn here. More miracles."

Egypt in the News During the Mission

After the mission, I found out for the first time about events that occurred while we were in Egypt. Here are the headlines and sources:

February 22, from the BBC: "Egyptian four-year-old's life sentence a mistake, military says," (https://www.bbc.com/news/world-middle-east-35633314). A 4-year-old was arrested by the police and sent away for a life sentence but later, the government decided that maybe the 4-year-old wasn't a mass murderer—maybe they'd made a mistake.

February 25, another BBC article: "Egypt's first convicted FGM doctor, Fadl, loses licence" (https://www.bbc.com/news/world-middle-east-35664978). This was a story about a 13-year-old girl dying after having an illegal female genital mutilation (FGM) procedure. According to internet information, 93% of women in Egypt have suffered from a Muslim ritual procedure called female genital mutilation. It is barbaric. It was outlawed even in Egypt in 2008. It is spoken against by the U.N., by the United States, by every civilized nation. Still, it is an accepted and widespread traditional practice in Egypt and other radical countries and is increasing in the U.K. and Scandinavia.

February 18, a third BBC article: "Egypt to shut prominent centre that documents torture" (https://www.bbc.com/news/world-middle-east-35600227). A center documenting specific cases of torture in Cairo was being shut down by the dictatorship.

Egypt in the News After the Trip

Over the next year, the internet was peppered with stories by the BBC and other European news sources about the Giulio Regeni news story.

A *BBC News* story was published on February 24, 2016, titled "Egypt: Italian's killers may have had revenge motive" (https://www.bbc.com/news/world-middle-east-35650418). The international media had suggested that Giulio Regeni's death may have been at the hands of the security forces, but Egyptian officials have dismissed this accusation against the dictator's corrupt police. Mr. Regeni was a graduate student of Cambridge University and had traveled to the American University in Cairo to research Egyptian trade agreements and labor rights, a very sensitive topic. His mutilated body was found dumped on the roadside on the outskirts of Cairo. Authorities said he had seven broken bones, signs of electrocution to his genitals, widespread trauma injuries, and a brain hemorrhage. His body was found naked from the waist down on the side of the road.

On Reuters.com, a March 1, 2016, article: "Exclusive: Italian killed in Egypt was interrogated for days - forensics expert" (https://www.reuters.com/article/us-egypt-italian-interrogation-exclusive-idUSKC-N0W33ZU). This article reported on how the Italian government sent over investigators and they studied his body. They stated that because of the burns with cigarettes in intervals over several days and based on the ages of the different bruises on his body and other evidence, it appeared he underwent three different interrogations. The signs are classic for the interrogation methods used by the Egyptian security forces. It pointed out that tensions were high between Egypt and Italy.

Then came the story "Italian prosecutor in Egypt to investigate student's torture, death" (https://www.thestar.com/news/world/2016/03/14/italian-prosecutor-in-egypt-to-investigate-

THE DOCTOR'S TRAVEL JOURNAL

students-torture-death.html), published on March 14, 2016, by the Associated Press, and written by Maggie Michael. The Italian foreign minister was quoted in this article, talking about how the Italian government was personally involved in trying to track down what truly happened.

Another article dated February 12, 2016, described how the family of the Italian Ph.D. student held a funeral in his hometown in Italy to pay tribute to him. It quoted colleagues of his, saying they were in shock over what happened to him (See "Giulio Regeni: Funeral held for Italian student killed in Cairo," https://www.bbc.com/news/world-europe-35561811).

On March 24, 2016, the BBC published a new story titled "Egypt 'finds killers of Italian student Giulio Regeni'" (https://www.bbc.com/news/world-middle-east-35897484). In that article, Egyptian police said they found the criminal gang that killed the Italian student in Cairo earlier that year. They raided a flat and killed everyone inside. The police disposed of their bodies and destroyed all evidence. They said that they were convinced those people were the murderers, so they were closing the case. I was highly suspicious when I read this about whether that was really what happened.

Financial Distress

Another news story about Egypt was "Egypt devalues pound, announces more flexible exchange rate policy" (https://www.reuters.com/article/us-egypt-currency/egypt-devalues-pound-announces-more-flexible-exchange-rate-policy-idUSKCN0WG1X7), from March 14, 2016. Tourism had been severely hit due to years of political turmoil. Because of that, they devalued their currency in order to stay afloat as a government.

BBC World News published an article on May 21, 2016, titled "Can Egypt's tourism recover from latest blow?" by Robert Plummer (https://www.bbc.com/news/business-36340581). Plummer wrote that before the fall of Mubarak during the 2011 Arab Spring, tourism brought $12.5 billion in revenue and employed one in 10 of the workforce. The pyramids and Red Sea resort of Sharm el-Sheikh brought 15 million tourists each year. Terrorists downed the Russian jet of tourists from the Sharm el-Sheikh in October 2015, killing 224. Another Red Sea resort, Hurghada, had terrorist stabbings in January 2016. Tourism brought only $6.1 billion in 2015 to Egypt and seemed to have shifted to Bulgaria and Spain.

Chaos

While all those terrible events were happening, this story came out on March 3, 2016, in *BBC News:* "Egyptian student faces U.S. deportation for Trump comment" (https://www.bbc.com/news/world-us-canada-35719470). It was about a college student in Orange, California, who made death threats against President Trump.

Daily News Egypt posted a story on March 16, 2016, and the headline was "Egypt doctors protest demanding legislative protection from assaults." Then on March 25, 2016, an article on the BBC was titled "Egypt unrest: Sisi warns over anti-government protests" (https://www.bbc.com/news/world-middle-east-36126691). In that article, the dictator warned against attempts to destabilize the state with anti-government protests. He said this to validate why he was cracking down on his citizens with the military. It also talked about Red Sea Island, which traditionally had been claimed as Egyptian property, being given to Saudi Arabia.

On May 23, 2016, there was another BBC story titled "Pope Francis meets top Sunni cleric after five-year freeze" (https://www.bbc.com/news/world-europe-36364478). It pictured the Pope with the top Sunni Muslim leader of the world, who is stationed in Cairo. They met, exchanged gifts and embraces, and "discussed conflicts and tensions between Christians and Muslims in the Middle East."

Violence

On July 13, 2016, there was an article on the BBC titled "Hundreds forcibly disappeared in Egypt crackdown, says Amnesty" (https://www.bbc.com/news/world-middle-east-36775035). It talked about children as young as 14 vanishing from the streets. It told story after story about how people were being blindfolded, handcuffed, and taken to be tortured and disappeared by the Egyptian security forces. That was according to Amnesty International.

"New accounts suggest severe torture in Egypt is ongoing" was an article published online by *Middle East Eye* (https://www.middleeasteye.net/features/new-accounts-suggest-severe-torture-egypt-ongoing). That article appeared on March 16, 2016, #EgyptTurmoil. It talked about new accounts of severe torture. It cited dozens of recent cases. It talked about electrocution. It documented individuals who died while in custody.

"Egypt explosion: Tourists on bus injured near Giza pyramids" (https://www.bbc.com/news/world-middle-east-48328793) was published on *BBC News* on May 19, 2019. A bomb targeted tourists on a bus. Seven South African tourists and 10 Egyptians were injured. This was the second bomb near the Great Pyramids in six months.

An article dated May 2, 2016, on *BBC News* was titled "Egypt violence: Three police killed in Cairo attack" (https://www.bbc.com/news/world-middle-east-39778169). The article described how "suspected militants" opened fire on a security convoy, killing three police in Cairo and wounding five others.

Another BBC story from August 4 was titled "Egypt 'kills head of IS branch in Sinai'" (https://www.bbc.com/news/world-middle-east-36978774). There was an ongoing war where the Islamic State (IS) and the Egyptian military were killing each other.

Smallpox Is One of the Plagues of Egypt

In preparation for a radio interview about vaccinations, I visited the CDC website. On their webpage about smallpox is a picture of the

3000-year-old mummy of Pharaoh Ramses the Fifth. The photo was provided to the CDC by the World Health Organization. The webpage explained that pustules containing smallpox organisms were discovered on the 3000-year-old remains.

Exodus 9:8 describes smallpox from head to toe as Divine judgement on the Egyptians. With the best medical care now available, smallpox would kill a third of victims. A smallpox epidemic would have had a much higher death rate 3000 years ago. I am amazed how, unwittingly, secular scientific organizations validate the historical Bible. Smallpox was eradicated via vaccines. Several nations have samples of live smallpox in secure labs.

Wars and Rumors of Wars

BBC News had an article on November 24, 2017, titled "Who are Egypt's militant groups?" (https://www.bbc.com/news/world-middle-east-34751349). The ISIS affiliate, Sinai Province, targets Christians and Sufi Muslims. Jund al-Islam, Al-Mourabitoun, Ansar al-Islam, Ajnad Misr, and Hasm were other terror groups discussed in the article. The Muslim Brotherhood and al-Qaeda were present as well.

Egypt in turmoil: a *BBC News* article titled "Egypt police killed in IS attack on Sinai checkpoint" (https://www.bbc.com/news/world-middle-east-48525868) was posted on June 5, 2019. Ten police were killed in simultaneous attacks of two checkpoints by ISIS. Attacks occurred on Eid al-Fitr, a Muslim religious holiday. Human Rights Watch reported war crimes by the Egyptian government. Arbitrary mass arrests, torture, extrajudicial killings, and air and ground attacks against civilians were reported. The article said the government denied these claims.

Photos Taken in Egypt

A recycling truck from Trash City.

Dr. Bartlett outside the Egyptian Museum in Cairo.

Dr. Bartlett inside the Egyptian Museum in Cairo.

The Nile River in Cairo.

Street vendors in Cairo.

Street vendors in Cairo.

Street vendors in Cairo.

Street vendors in Cairo.

Street vendors in Cairo.

Cave church in Egypt.

View from Mokatum.

Argentina Photos

Grant laying hands and praying for people.

Praying together for a miracle pregnancy: I have been waiting for you.

CHAPTER 3

Global Cabal—Evil Is Being Exposed

Have nothing to do with the fruitless deeds of darkness, but rather expose them. **It is shameful even to mention** what the disobedient do in secret.

—Ephesians 5:11-12 NIV (emphasis added)

Call of God

I received an email from the World Missions Alliance listing upcoming mission opportunities. I felt immediately called to go to Argentina in October of 2016. My wife had read the email separately from me and told me she felt we were meant to go on the Argentina trip. We felt the call at the same time, even though we were not in the same place. In agreement, we decided we would take our 8-year-old son with us on this mission trip. We bought our airline tickets and were ready to go.

During a church service our pastor, Mark Bristow, spoke about going to the tip of Argentina on prior mission trips. We found out we were going to the same church congregation that Mark had visited. When God gives direction, He will also confirm it. This was the confirmation.

Matthew 18:16 NIV:

" . . . every matter may be established by the testimony of two or three witnesses."

THE DOCTOR'S TRAVEL JOURNAL

2 Corinthians 13:1 NIV:

" . . . Every matter must be established by the testimony of two or three witnesses."

Deuteronomy 19:15 NIV:

. . . A matter must be established by the testimony of two or three witnesses.

Argentina in the News

I told my wife I was realizing there is a global network of evil, with activities in Argentina, Egypt, and Europe. Nazi Germany of WWII, the police state of Egypt, Middle Eastern terrorism, and the atrocities in South America over the last 60 years were all connected. They were not separate islands of evil. We watched a History Channel special about Nazis going to Argentina. I told her about related articles I had come across.

A *BBC News* article on June 13, 2000, was titled "Argentina 'sorry' over Nazis" (http://news.bbc.co.uk/2/hi/americas/789756.stm). In the article, the president of Argentina apologized for creating a hiding place for Nazi war criminals during World War II. More than 150 Nazi leaders, including Adolf Eichmann, who was considered the chief architect of the holocaust, were allowed sanctuary in Argentina. It went on to say that Argentina allowed them sanctuary and basically gave them protected status, even though they were often involved in criminal activity.

On March 22, 2015, there was another article on *BBC News* titled "Argentine archeologists probe 'Nazi hideout' for clues." They found whole towns in remote jungle areas in Argentina controlled by the Nazis. The Nazis lived there and the villagers spoke German. They found many Nazi Germany coins from the 1930s and 1940s, and they found evidence that these towns were made for the Nazis to allow them to hide out and keep functioning after World War II.

The documentary I saw on the History Channel covered "Scarface" Skorzeny. Otto Skorzeny was the Nazi leader who formalized terrorism and wrote a manual on how to recruit and train terrorists. His manual explained how to organize terrorist cells so they can operate independently and not be shut down. After World War II, he supposedly "escaped" from prison and went to Argentina because the dictator of Argentina was a Nazi sympathizer. Afterward, he was welcomed to Egypt as a war hero.

While Argentina openly let these Nazis in, they didn't stop there. Argentina shares a long and porous border with Chile and, as I widened my search, it became clear that there were Nazis in Chile as well.

BBC News had an article on October 4, 2000, called "Chilean police raid German enclave" (http://news.bbc.co.uk/2/hi/americas/968574.stm). It described several German communities with Nazi leaders in them who arrived there after the holocaust. Some of them were later arrested and brought to justice. One of the communities had 13,000 hectares of land close to the mountains. BBC said it was a closed community with its own hospital and school. Many of the Nazi leaders were accused of child sex abuse and scientific experiments studying the effects of torture on their victims. The twisted Nazi experiments had continued after World War II.

On March 11, 2005, there was a *BBC News* article titled "Secrets of ex-Nazi's Chilean fiefdom" (http://news.bbc.co.uk/2/hi/americas/4340591.stm), by Becky Banford. It stated that a former Nazi medic and accused cult leader was captured in Argentina after eight years on the run. While in Argentina, he had set up a youth home, purportedly to care for war orphans. After he was charged for sexually abusing boys, he fled to Chile where he set up a colony with other Nazis, called Colonia Dignidad. They operated for decades there.

Another article came out of Chile on May 24, 2011, about the same Nazi colony: "Colonia Dignidad cult suspects arrested in Chile" (https://www.bbc.com/news/world-latin-america-13535187). Some of the German Nazi leaders who were there were arrested and accused of kidnapping, manslaughter, sexually abusing children, and membership of an illicit organization. They were, of course, Nazis and Nazi sympathizers.

101

Published on July 13, 2016, an article on *BBC News* was titled "Germany deplores rights violations at enclave in Chile" (https://www.bbc.com/news/world-latin-america-36780312). In that article, the German president condemned the human rights violations at the secretive colony of ethnic Germans in Chile in the 1960s and 1970s. Children and young people were physically and psychologically abused. Germany promised to release the classified documents that it had on the colony in April.

Buenos Aires

In September 2016, my wife, 8-year-old son, and I emerged from the jetway into the Buenos Aires airport. Overhead announcements of flights droned in Spanish as travelers hurried past others waiting at gates. It was muggy in the airport and, after the long flight from Houston, we were ready for a shower and fresh clothes.

We waited for our luggage, then worked our way through the crowds to exit the airport. It was hot and humid, but we enjoyed the slight breeze hitting our face. I noticed a rough-looking, unshaven, middle-aged Latino man leaning against the airport wall. He was wearing a worn-out short-sleeve shirt and jeans. He was smoking and glaring at three elderly black women who had surrounded him. I had heard about the three sisters from Jamaica who had been missionaries for over 40 years.

The eldest sister, Ivy Barrett, was 90 years old at the time of this mission. The two younger sisters, Daphne Lindo and Lilla Lindo Wallace, were 89-year-old twins. This had to be them. I moved closer to hear what was going on. They were smiling, giggling, and speaking in a singsong style. When one started talking the other would finish her sentence. It was obvious they had just met the stranger and were telling him about Jesus. Soon, they were singing in a three-part harmony.

Several people started gathering around them to listen and watch. The sisters showed no reservations to praise the Lord. The man's scowl turned to a toothy grin from ear to ear. He couldn't keep the tough-guy persona any longer. The sisters prayed a blessing over him on the busy curb. He gave them each a hug. Helen Todd appeared out of the terminal and she waved the sisters over to join us. Other mission team members gathered, including Lynn and Marie Bailey from Oregon, who were on the Iraq 2014 mission with me. They were witnesses to the multiple people delivered from demons in Iraq.

We took a taxi to our hotel in Buenos Aires. An elderly white lady, with the classic senior hair-do and glasses, wearing a jogging suit, was in the hotel lobby. It was Margaret, an 80-year-old lady whom my middle son and I had met in October 2014 on our mission trip to the Republic of Georgia. She'd had a stroke, so walking was a big challenge for her. She said she was in pain, but she was not letting her poor health hold her back. If anyone had the right to complain or bow out of this trip gracefully, it was her. Margaret expressed that God had called her to Argentina; she had no plans not to complete her race.

We had the evening to recover before the connecting flight the next morning. Margaret wanted to take a walk and see the sights, so we joined her for a walk around several of the city parks. Much of the architecture reminded me of Paris. In fact, Buenos Aires is often called 'the Paris of South America.'

The Andes Mountains

We all flew together to Ushuaia the next morning. After several hours, we saw the majestically snowcapped Andes Mountains outside the plane window. There was some expected turbulence. The sisters sat across the aisle and were audibly praying. Hearing their prayers mitigated any fear caused by the turbulence. Surely, we were under God's protection.

Planes have to drop altitude rapidly from over the Andes Mountains in order to land on a short airstrip next to the ocean. The landing had some rodeo effects. Chuck Todd told us later that his plane could not make the landing at its first pass and had to pull up and make a second run. Once we had gathered our luggage, we left the Ushuaia airport.

The scenery was breathtaking. White-haloed mountains surrounded the airport. The crisp air smelled clean and fresh and the city was alive with hope and energy. Just traveling from the airport to our hotel, it was clear Ushuaia was experiencing a financial renaissance of sorts. New buildings, hotels, and shopping destinations were being built everywhere. There was even a whole city block zoned off for a new Hard Rock Cafe.

God's Timing

When we arrived, we met the rest of the mission team. Chuck Todd led the team orientation. We found out that the pastor who invited Chuck to bring the mission team was in Spain. He had been lobbying Chuck and Helen to bring a team to his congregation for the last three years. Weeks before we arrived, the pastor suddenly resigned from being the pastor of his Ushuaia congregation. He oversaw many churches in Spain and he decided that God wanted him to stay in Spain, so he was not coming back to join us at the church that he had invited us to visit.

The congregation was in shock because they did not foresee their pastor leaving. The atmosphere was one of confusion, loss, and disappointment. This pastor had started his congregation 25 years ago and was the only pastor the church had ever known. Again, it was perfect timing for a mission trip by the World Missions Alliance. We were just what the congregation and the city needed, since a replacement pastor had not been chosen yet.

The Land of Fire

Tierra Del Fuego is the Spanish name for "Land of Fire," which is what they call the archipelago off the southernmost tip of Argentina and Chile. It was named by the European settlers due to sightings from the sea of the many bonfires built by the natives. Magellan found the area in 1520. Ushuaia is on the main island.

Spiritual Revival

There was an evening service the first night we arrived. Helen spoke and gave a sermon. Then the team was invited up front to pray with anyone in need. My son stayed next to me as a prayer partner during the time of ministry. A 12-year-old boy named Dylan was the first to come forward for prayer. As soon as we started praying he fell to the ground, speaking in tongues. I was surprised; Dylan was tearful and trembling. The whole congregation had eyes on the boy as he cried and spoke in tongues. Others streamed forward for prayer. Soon, the atmosphere was electric; with many people praying, some falling to the ground under the influence of the Holy Spirit: the fire of revival.

The next night, the crowd had increased until it was standing room only. Helen asked my son if he would play his violin and my wife accompanied him on the keyboard. They played "Great I Am" twice, while the mission team sang in English. To my surprise, the congregation joined in and sang the songs in Spanish at the same time. It was a powerful experience. The mission team came to the altar at the end of the service to pray with anyone who came forward. There were more prayers and tears, and some people were falling under the influence of the Holy Spirit.

Pray for Those Who Have Hurt You

Matthew 5:43-45 NIV:

> "You have heard that it was said, 'Love your neighbor and hate your enemy.' But I tell you, love your enemies and pray for those who persecute you, that you may be children of your Father in heaven. He causes his sun to rise on the evil and good, and sends rain on the righteous and the unrighteous."

At the third evening service, I spoke about praying for your enemies. I pointed out that Jesus made a distinction between forgiving your enemies, in Matthew 6:14-15, and praying for your enemies, in Matthew 5:43-45.

I told my story of being woken up at 4:00 a.m. and hearing, "Pray for those who have despitefully used you." I prayed for the first three people who came to mind: my son-in-law and his parents. I gave a summary of the events that related to that prayer. I also told how the Lord had recently reconciled my brother and father after eight years of estrangement. I encouraged the congregation to pray for their enemies so the spirit of reconciliation could be manifest in their congregation, city, and families.

The mission team came forward to the altar and was overwhelmed with people coming forward for prayer. Many were waiting in line quite a while to find an available missions team member to join them in prayer.

I prayed with a man who had gone through a divorce and whose three children had gone in three different directions. It sounded like his family had just exploded. He was heartbroken. But the Spirit of Reconciliation was breathing on Ushuaia. After the service, my son told my wife and I that, during the corporate worship, he had a vision. He saw giant chains falling off of his sister who had become estranged to our family.

The Three Sisters

The three sisters from Jamaica came forward to give their testimony at the fourth evening service. All of the seats were full, and every square inch had someone standing from the community at large. The sisters told about a mission trip they took when they were in their 40s. They were sent by their church missions board to a remote African tribe: the Kaonde of Zambia. One of the younger twins was a trained midwife. When they arrived at the dry, dusty village, a hostile witch doctor and the village elders greeted them.

The village elders could not understand how the second twin of the sisters was still alive. They had never seen a second twin live to adulthood. They had a term for the second twin, "kapya." They believed that the second twin had evil spirits. The tribe had a tradition for hundreds of years that the mother would wrap the second twin on her back when it was six days old and carry it to the river. She would then untie the carrying blanket and let the baby fall in the river and be swept away. The tribe's elders became more aggressive and hostile toward the three sisters.

The sisters had no male escorts, police, or soldiers to protect them. A righteous indignation rose up in the sisters and they started preaching to the tribe's elders. The tribe's elders repented of murdering the second twins of their tribe and they repented their witchcraft. The whole tribe became a Christian tribe and the sisters continued to live with the Kaonde for five years, without electricity or running water. The youngest twin sister delivered all of the village babies for those five years. God used a second twin to break the curse that led to the death of second twins for hundreds of years. It was a story of family members killing family members.

After the ladies gave their testimony, the mission team came to the front so they could once again be available to pray with people. The front of the service was packed with people wanting prayer. The divorced gentleman I prayed with the evening before was excited to introduce me to his oldest son, who had joined him for that service. The man who had been so lonely had been reunited with two people in his family. Again, it was powerful ministry.

A Child Shall Lead Them

The next evening's service focused on the children. The local congregation had been preparing a drama to perform before the church. The children's program had been promoted in the city, so the church was packed. Christians and non-Christians alike, people from all parts of the city were present. Some of the children in the presentation had parents there who had never come to church and many that were not Christian. The children acted out their drama with great passion. They wore costumes of angels worshipping God in Heaven while music played over the speakers.

Kurt and Margaret Gorton presented the Good News. I had worked with Kurt before on the mission to Nepal. They were followed by my son playing the violin while my wife played the keyboard. They played "Great I Am" and "It Is Well" as Kurt gave an altar call. Thirty children came forward to accept Jesus. As the music continued, a wave of adults followed the children to the altar to accept Jesus into their hearts.

I've Been Waiting for You

My wife was asked to give the message for the next evening service. She explained that we had planned on having birth children and adopting children, but her appendix ruptured a year after we were married. The doctors told her she would never be pregnant, but she knew God could do anything. She hoped and prayed that she would have a baby. We adopted six children and each child was an individual miracle and an answer to a prayer. She described how, month after month, she waited for a miracle pregnancy. She had received prophecies that she would have a birth child but, she explained, as time passed she felt that her hopes and dreams of a pregnancy were slipping away. She felt helpless.

Then, after 20 years of marriage and turning 40 years old, she started feeling poorly. She told the congregation that she had started experiencing dizziness and trouble concentrating. She was worried that she might have a brain tumor. An MRI was scheduled because it is more accurate than a CAT scan. The radiology center had signs posted stating that patients should tell the rad tech if they might be pregnant because of danger to the baby.

Although she wanted to be pregnant, she had 20 years of marriage and no pregnancy. She had not missed a menstrual period. She lay on the MRI table but as the table was being slid into the MRI tube she panicked. Repeated attempts to stay in the tight space of the MRI were unsuccessful due to intense claustrophobia. The radiology techs confessed that they could not stand to have an MRI either, due to claustrophobia.

The plan was changed and she had a CAT scan performed instead. When she entered her car in the parking lot of the CAT scan location she turned on the radio. A lady was telling her story about getting a CAT scan. The doctors thought the woman had a tumor but instead they found out she was pregnant. She wondered if that could happen with her. Her CAT scan came back normal.

Several days later, she did a home pregnancy test that was positive. She used to think that every month her dreams and hopes for answered prayers were moving farther away from manifesting. Now she understood that her dream and answered prayer was moving closer every month. She told the congregation that what God had done for her, He could do for them. The mission team came to the front to pray for any needs among the congregation. Many people came forward for ministry and prayer. She waited quietly for someone to come ask her to pray with them. She was convinced that God had someone she was supposed to meet. She watched as most of the people prayed with other mission team members.

Finally, a woman who appeared to be around 30 years old with a ponytail, casual sweater, and jeans timidly approached her.

My wife said, "I've been waiting a long time for you."

With tears in her eyes, the woman said to my wife, "I have been waiting a long time for you too." The woman explained that she'd had five miscarriages, and her prayer was to have a healthy pregnancy and baby. The women cried and prayed together in that holy atmosphere.

Penguin Island

My son and I invited Dylan to take a boat tour to Penguin Island with us during the day. It was amazing. We passed the southernmost lighthouse on the globe and saw an island covered with sea lions and an island covered with commodores. Finally, we arrived at Penguin Island. We were thrilled to see three species of penguins on the island from the boat. There were over 100 penguins playing in the water, sitting on eggs, and waddling around on the island. It was a great day.

Final Night

The word of our work there had spread throughout the town and the final evening service had even more people than before. After the sermon, the mission team members once again came to the front to be available for prayer. Like every other night's service, my son stayed next to me. We were a prayer team. I was holding a cup of olive oil so we could anoint people and pray for them together.

Two elderly women were standing together, quietly waiting on the front row. They were wearing conservative dresses with their hair pulled back, very prim and proper. They motioned for my son to come and lay his hands on them and pray for them. He dipped his little fingers in the bowl of oil and reached as high as he could, so he could touch the first lady's forehead. She fell back into her folding chair in a daze. We moved on to the second lady and the same thing happened; she fell back in the chair. My son was smaller than them and he did not push them.

After the service, the first lady came and found us with the translator. She explained that when he touched her forehead she felt fire come from the top of her head, down to her hip that was hurting, and the pain went away. She said she had an artificial hip from a hip replacement years ago and that she had been in severe, constant pain for months. I encouraged her to tell the congregation what had happened. She worked her way to the front of the church and grabbed the microphone. She got everyone's attention and told what had happened. The crowd cheered.

Psalm 107:2 NIV:

> Let the redeemed of the Lord tell their story—those he redeemed from the hand of the foe.

The gentleman who had gone through divorce had two sons sitting next to him in the back row of the church. After the service, I came back to talk to them, and I told his sons the Best News in the world. They both prayed, asking Jesus to be Lord of their lives. Now this family had three members who were reunited.

Psalm 133:1 TLB:

> How wonderful it is, how pleasant, when brothers live in harmony!

Divine Connections

One of the Argentina mission team members was named Diane. She explained to my wife that her son graduated from Full Sail University. Full Sail is the premier school for computer animation and digital graphics. My wife explained that our youngest daughter had a dream of doing computer animation and digital graphics. We were concerned that our daughter's chances for enrollment would be limited because she was homeschooled. Diane gave my wife the contact information for her son in Detroit, since he still occasionally taught classes at Full Sail in addition to running a successful business creating sound effects for movies: his company was called the Detroit Chop Shop.

When we got home, my wife called Diane's son and he was very encouraging. He explained that the admissions coordinator for Full Sail University was his good friend. He promised he would call his friend and discuss our daughter's interest in attending Full Sail. My wife later spoke with the admissions advisor and he was also very positive and encouraging. We found out that Full Sail has an online degree plan, which she enrolled in and is currently attending. God's "right time" and "right place" for relationships that would open doors of opportunity were beyond what we could have anticipated. We did not go to Argentina with the intent to fulfill our daughter's career dream, but so it happened. God is faithful.

Acts 1:8 NIV:

> "But you will receive power when the Holy Spirit comes on you; and you will be my witnesses in Jerusalem, and in all Judea and Samaria, and to the ends of the earth."

End of the World

The tip of Argentina is called "Fin Del Mundo" which translates to "The End of the World." God can give you the desires of your heart even at the end of the world.

When you are led by the Lord to minister to a specific need, i.e., reconciliation, the Lord will often meet the same need for you. Now, my daughter and son-in law are in a peaceful relationship with the family. God has granted peace between the son-in-law's parents and our family as well.

Psalm 34:10 NIV:

> The lions may grow weak and hungry, but those who seek the Lord lack no good thing.

Psalm 84:11 NIV:

> For the Lord God is a sun and shield; the Lord bestows favor and honor; no good does he withhold from those whose walk is blameless.

Matthew 6:33 NIV:

> But seek first his kingdom and his righteousness, and all these things will be given to you as well.

Clues of the Global Evil Network

John 3:19-20 NIV:

> This is the verdict: Light has come into the world, but people loved darkness instead of light because their deeds were evil. Everyone who does evil hates the light, and will not come into the light for fear that their deeds will be exposed.

The pattern of child abuse by people in religious organizations is internationally widespread and goes back for generations. In recent years, many predators have been brought into the light and some have been convicted and removed from their positions. The list is long. A few examples follow, and more can be found in Appendix I.

"Fifty children saved as international paedophile ring busted" was a *BBC News* article published on May 23, 2019 (https://www.bbc.com/news/world-48379983). Arrests were made in the U.S., Thailand, and Australia. Operation Black Wrist was an Interpol investigation focused on the dark web. The U.S. Homeland Security traced the IP address of the website. Thousands of photos and videos of children being tortured were on the website.

An article titled "Cardinal George Pell loses appeal against sexual abuse convictions" was published on *BBC News* on August 21, 2019 (https://www.bbc.com/news/world-australia-49416573). Pell was the most senior Catholic cleric to be convicted in Australia of rape of little boys. He was in charge of the Catholic money and number two in power under the Pope.

In "Pope Francis tells gay Chilean sex abuse victim 'God loves you'" (*BBC News*, May 22, 2018: https://www.bbc.com/news/world-latin-america-44215996), the victim says that Pope Francis told him 'God made you this way.'

From *BBC News* on November 25, 2019, "Argentina: Catholic priests jailed for abusing deaf children" reports on how priests abused kids in Italy and then were moved to Argentina to engage in organized sexual abuse of deaf kids (https://www.bbc.com/news/world-latin-america-50549918). Children were not taught sign language, so they could not tell. The catholic organization did not acknowledge, investigate, or intervene. It was the Argentina police that shut it down. This was while Pope Francis was Cardinal of Argentina. He was responsible for oversight. Pope Francis can't say, "Not on my watch."

"Pope Francis: 'About 2%' of Catholic clergy paedophiles" was a *BBC News* article title on July 13, 2014 (https://www.bbc.com/news/world-europe-28282050).

"Dark web child abuse: Hundreds arrested across 38 countries," published by *BBC News* on October 18, 2019, described that the web site had more than 200,000 videos of child torture and abuse. Arrests of some of the perpetrators were made in the U.K., Ireland, U.S., South Korea, Germany, Spain, Saudi Arabia, UAE, Canada, and others. Infants, toddlers, and children were victims in videos (https://www.bbc.com/news/world-50073092).

"Former Anglican dean jailed for raping boy in Australia," published by *BBC News* on October 17, 2019 (https://www.bbc.com/news/world-australia-50077792). The second-most senior Australian religious figure was convicted of child sexual abuse.

Other related articles on *BBC News* include "Australia's Anglican church gets 1,115 child abuse complaints" (https://www.bbc.com/news/world-australia-39299861); and "Australia child abuse inquiry finds 'serious failings'" (https://www.bbc.com/news/world-australia-42361874).

Defending Children

James 1:27 NIV:

> Religion that God our Father accepts as pure and faultless is this: to look after orphans and widows in their distress and to keep oneself from being polluted by the world.

As Texas television station CBS7 News Medical Expert, I organized a five-part series on sex trafficking of children. Sheriff Painter of Midland County, Sheriff Griffis of Ector County, Sheriff Aguilar of Crane County, and Dr. Greg Romine of Called to Rescue were the panel of experts. Tips were given to the viewing audience on how to recognize and report victims. Tips on how to prevent children from becoming victims were provided. Check out CalledtoRescue.org and SharedHope.org for more information.

A local Texas pastor, Pastor Russ Nebhut, is author of *I'm Still Here by the Grace of God: The Story of an Adult Survivor of Childhood Sexual Abuse and His Journey to Wholeness*, available on Amazon.

The President Takes Action

"My administration will focus on ending the absolutely horrific practice of human trafficking." —President Donald Trump

The President's Interagency Task Force to Monitor and Combat Trafficking in Persons was created by President Trump. He appointed survivors to the Advisory Council on Human Trafficking. In 2017, Trump issued an executive order to crack down on transnational human trafficking rings.

As a result, 1,500 arrests and 530 convictions were made, over 500 victims freed, and 42 criminal enterprises dismantled. The Department of Justice assisted more than 8,000 survivors between July 2016 and June 2017.

CHAPTER 4

Destinies and Dreams

Sing to God, sing in praise of his name,
extol him who rides on the clouds;
rejoice before him—his name is the Lord.
A father to the fatherless, a defender of widows,
is God in his holy dwelling.
God sets the lonely in families,
he leads out the prisoners with singing;
but the rebellious live in a sun-scorched land.
—Psalm 68:4-6 NIV

Morgan Wei Wan

2014, Texas Tech University
Lubbock, Texas

The Asian lady teaching the college class had nodded and smiled at Morgan Wei Wan, a petite Chinese college student, when she entered the room. Morgan settled into a wooden seat in the front row of the auditorium; she chose the front row so she could hear and see everything perfectly. When she looked around, she saw the usual cowboys in the back row, their boots perched on the seatbacks in front of them. She was one of the few in the Mandarin class at Texas Tech University who was not Caucasian.

She smiled, certain she was going ace that class. Why not? She was born in China, for crying out loud! Mandarin was her native tongue until she was adopted and moved to Texas at 4 years old. All that was a distant memory now. She could hear and see well but she wasn't going to take a chance on missing anything in that class. It was *her* class. She owned it!

English was a distant second language for the young Chinese teacher. She awkwardly tried to explain that she was going to teach the class a common Chinese nursery rhyme with accompanying hand gestures. As she began to teach, she looked at Morgan in shock.

"You know this song?" she asked Morgan in Mandarin.

Morgan looked down at her hands that were moving in front of her as she continued to complete the song. In that moment, the classroom dissolved and she was a little girl in the orphanage once again. Tears streamed down her face, while in the flashback she saw and heard the other kids in the orphanage singing and moving their hands; she was not able to stop the flow of images. The class just sat and watched silently as Morgan seemed to be in another world.

That was the first of many flashbacks to her early childhood in a Chinese orphanage. The gaps in her memory were being filled. Wei Wan, at 4 years old, still lived in a crib with a series of crib mates in the same orphanage where she had lived since infancy. As crib mates died, they were replaced. The children were never allowed outside the room. All the little girls had bobbed haircuts and were small due to malnutrition. The female orphanage workers came in the room twice a day to feed the kids a cup of white rice or a bowl of green soup—always the same food. Sometimes a kid was rewarded with an almond cookie if she was successful at potty training. A very small room next to "the room" had a cooking pot, which served as the toilet.

The orphans had no possessions except the clothes on their backs. The room was often cold, and many mornings began with orphanage workers arriving to cover the bodies of dead children with sheets. If a child was not doing well, the workers would simply not feed her in order to save her rations for the orphans who appeared strong and able to survive.

Wei Wan assumed the role of "mother hen" for the other orphans in the room. At night, she would often climb out of her crib to pillage the kitchen. She would push another crib under a window in the wall between rooms, then she would put the empty toilet pot in the crib to stand on, and climb through the window into the kitchen. She would fill the pot with cookies, rice, and any clothes she could find, and then pass them out to her roommates. The room was poorly lit, and the kids would attempt to hide food and clothes under their crib mattresses.

Wei Wan was labeled a troublemaker by the workers and was often scolded and punished. The other orphans told her she was the bravest. They looked up to her, and she would tell them to be brave. She told them to act strong and healthy, so food and clothes would not be withheld from them. She had a series of crib mates during the four years she spent there.

Second Chances

Texas, 1992

My wife and I applied to adopt an infant from China before we had any children. Our INS-600 application was approved after the FBI checked our fingerprints and backgrounds. The packet containing birth and marriage certificates, social worker home studies, letters of reference, tax returns, etc., was notarized. We then had to mail the notarized documents to the state capital to be certified. The same packet was then mailed to the Chinese consulate in Houston to be authenticated. The back and forth mailing process took over a month. The day we mailed the packet to Houston, CNN reported breaking news that China had closed its doors to international adoption. We felt so defeated!

Four years later, after adopting two infants, we applied to China again, which had reinstated international adoption. We saw a picture of a 4-year-old girl on the waiting orphans webpage of Children's Hope International Adoption Agency. She was considered a special needs orphan and considered difficult to place because she was older. Most people were hoping to adopt infants. We believe she was supposed to be our daughter all along. We were told her name was Wei Wan. As an infant, she had been left on the steps of a police station in a box with a note. No relative had checked on her for the last four years. We wanted her.

At last, the paperwork was finalized and everything was in order. The adoption agency suggested that we send our pictures and a toy to the little girl. The orphanage director told the adoption agency that she would like a Barbie doll. Dawn and I searched for several days to find a Chinese Barbie doll and then were told that she wanted a doll with yellow hair. We mailed a package of clothes, a Barbie doll, and pictures of our family to Wei Wan's orphanage. We received a picture in return of Wei Wan holding our picture and her new doll.

Years later, after Morgan had experienced flashbacks in her Mandarin class, she told us that when a kid was about to be adopted, the orphanage workers would bathe her for the first time in her life. When she received her first bath, she was also told her name for the first time. She remembered the workers were surprised that her crib mate, Wei Wa, had a similar name. The orphans did not know their own names or the names of any of their fellow orphans because the workers had never spoken their names.

Morgan remembered they had always been hungry. Due to their impending adoptions, they were fed extra food and lined up on a couch to receive gifts from the waiting parents. The orphanage sent pictures of the occasion to the adoption agency. That was her first "party" ever. They had never had birthday parties or celebrated Chinese New Year, or any other holiday, before. She decided during the party that she would no longer be "mother hen" to the other orphans. No longer would she steal food, because she did not want to get in trouble and miss something new that was happening. She remembered all the orphans who were left behind, crying and asking her not to leave them. One sickly girl, especially, stands out in her memory to this day.

Challenges

Dawn and I had scheduled our flights to China to adopt Wei Wan when we got a call that there had been a bizarre interruption. The Chinese government had recently started a foster care program for orphans. A family took Wei Wan on a day trip away from the orphanage, but they had not brought her back. It was a time of prayer and soul-searching. The embarrassed orphanage director offered to reassign a new orphan to our family. The agency said this had never happened before.

We still believed that Wei Wan was meant to be in our family, so we kept praying and didn't give up. Two weeks later, Wei Wan was returned to the orphanage. The Chinese orphanage director was amazed and excited that it had worked out. She hinted that maybe the foster family kept Wei Wan so long because they knew she was going to the U.S., and they had heard terrible things about the U.S. They did not want her to go to that "terrible" place. They had no other ties to Wei Wan otherwise. The American adoption agency workers were excited that, against all odds, it had worked out well.

On February 2, 2014, Wei Wan finally explained to Dawn and me what had happened. Wei Wan had left the orphanage for the first time with some strangers, the foster family, who brought her to the city. Morgan had never been around crowds of people in public before. The new noises and sights were overwhelming. Wei Wan got separated from the couple and continued to ride the city bus. She was eventually dropped off in the country and left alone for hours. She remembered seeing chickens and farm animals for the first time.

Eventually, an orphanage worker tracked her down and gave her a bicycle ride to an older lady who was in the foster system. That was the first time she had felt the wind on her face. Wei Wan was returned to the orphanage and the adoption was back on track.

Shortly before we were ready to fly to China, Dawn developed symptoms of a severe bladder infection. She had never had a bladder infection before, and the symptoms were not resolving with antibiotics. She was afraid to leave the country in pain without knowing medical care was secure in China. After much prayer, in pain, and without assurance that she could receive good medical care in China, Dawn trusted Jesus and boarded the plane (bringing along the antibiotics).

New Family

Jeremiah 29:11 NIV:

"For I know the plans I have for you," declares the Lord, "plans to give you a hope and a future."

We flew to Japan, then to Beijing, and finally Nanjing. We were told we could not visit the orphanage, but that our daughter would be brought to our hotel. The orphanage director and one of her helpers brought Wei Wan from the orphanage to our hotel.

Dawn had arranged little girl dresses, hair bows, shoes, and more on display while we anxiously awaited Wei Wan's arrival. Dawn would rearrange, count, and study the clothes for flaws as the hours passed. You would have thought she was the new manager of a clothing store, expecting corporate to come inspect the store!

Finally, there was a knock on the hotel door. A three-foot-tall Chinese girl with a bob haircut pushed past the three Chinese women and burst through the doorway with a smile from ear to ear, about to pop from excitement. A constant stream of squeals of excitement were punctuated with exclamations in Mandarin and rolls of laughter. The little girl could not contain her joy!

Her twinkling eyes were under eyebrows as thick as caterpillars. Her cheeks were abnormally red with makeup in an attempt to conceal a dark scar on her right cheek. She ran in a monkey-like way, because of rickets bowing her legs, straight to Dawn and wrapped her in a big bear hug. When Wei Wan's eyes spotted the wrapped presents on the bed, she erupted in more squeals and giggles. Wrapping paper was flying. She wanted to try on all the clothes at once; three layers of new clothes were on before she slowed down. In contrast to Wei Wan, buzzing around the room in loud, overflowing delight, the orphanage director spoke in hushed tones to our translator.

Through the translator we heard superficial, vague info about the orphanage, Wei Wan, and her friends. Dawn gave Wei Wan the choice of her future American name. Wei Wan would pick her new American first name. The translator said Wei Wan wanted to see the names spelled out. With a wide grin, nodding as she looked from person to person, she tapped her finger on the paper lying before her. Morgan it was! The orphanage workers left, with bows and smiles, after an hour. Morgan stayed with us the remainder of the trip.

Crib Mates Get New Lives

Morgan Wei Wan's crib mate from the orphanage was adopted at the same time by Florence Abrams. Florence was a Jewish New York attorney who had an adopted daughter from El Salvador. Florence was compassionate but she had street smarts. It was a pleasure going through the process in China side-by-side as she adopted Wei Wa, who became Jessica. We quickly learned how to communicate with the girls through pointing and charades. Morgan Wei Wan, Dawn, and I flew from Nanjing to Guangzhou, which is where the U.S. Consulate is located. The paperwork was completed. Morgan now had a visa to travel to America.

Sham Exam

Morgan underwent a series of medical exams by Chinese healthcare workers at the consulate clinics. It was a very superficial exam, but with much ado. The doctors and workers wore all white attire from the U.S. 1950s, complete with cloth caps and masks. The equipment was from

123

THE DOCTOR'S TRAVEL JOURNAL

the same era; the large round mirror on the forehead to reflect light was used to examine her ears. Morgan was reported to be in perfect health.

After the long trip home, Morgan Wei Wan blended instantly with our family. Several months later, Morgan tried to copy our daughter, Julia, age 3, doing a cartwheel in the living room. Morgan's arm snapped due to vitamin deficiencies. I set her forearm bones and placed a cast on her arm. Though a year older than her new siblings, Morgan was considerably lighter due to the poor nutrition. We found that Morgan was sneaking food out of the pantry at night and hiding it under her bed and in her closet. She had learned hoarding and survival skills in the orphanage.

Help Comes When You Need It

We would take the family to Chinese restaurants, hoping to preserve Morgan's ability to speak Mandarin. Morgan would listen to the Chinese ladies speak Mandarin but refused to respond in Mandarin. She would answer in English or with nods and gestures. When asked about her past, she would never recall anything prior to meeting us in China. Morgan always spoke very loudly and, after a short time in Texas, Morgan had green drainage come out of her ear. She had no pain. I brought her to my office and looked in her ears to find she had no eardrums! She had apparently had so many severe ear infections that her eardrums had rotted.

I asked Dr. Robert Byers, a professor of the M.D. Anderson Head and Neck Surgery Department, what ENT he recommended. He recommended Dr. Dan Franklin, who had recently placed tubes in his grandson's ears.

Eventually, we drove the nine-hour road trip to Houston multiple times, resulting in two surgeries for Morgan. New eardrums were created out of temporal fascia from behind her ears. Two weeks after the surgeries, testing revealed that Morgan had normal hearing! It was a miracle. Dr. Dan Franklin never charged us for the excellent care and surgeries.

God's Green Light to Go

Twenty years after coming home to us from China, Morgan had grown into an incredible, and deeply spiritual, young woman. World Missions Alliance has a contest for young people to win a free mission trip. They call it the Timothy Project. Morgan entered the contest with a one-minute video about why she felt called to missions.

Morgan was speechless and burst into tears of joy when she learned she had won a free mission trip to China. Twenty years before, when we adopted Morgan, the translator who helped Dawn and me in China said Morgan was possibly older than the stated age. She explained that many documents were inaccurate because the orphans were just abandoned. For that reason, we changed the year of her birth date by one year during the re-adoption process in Texas, as well as her subsequent passports. As a result, her current passport and original Chinese passport and birth certificates have different birth dates.

We were concerned that the birth certificate issue may cause problems in China if Morgan returned. We were not comfortable with Morgan going there with that issue unresolved. She applied for a visa through a company in Washington, D.C. that World Missions Alliance normally used for trips to China. Morgan's original Chinese passports, birth certificates, and documents, along with our adoption paperwork from the United States, were required to be mailed to the visa company so China could authenticate the records.

The owner of the visa company told World Missions Alliance that he was concerned about the birth date discrepancy. He told them he did not want to attempt to get a visa for Morgan. I called and spoke with him, and he said he would try to help. All of Morgan's important documents were mailed to the visa office in Washington, DC. We were relieved when all of Morgan's important documents were returned to us prior to the trip. Morgan was adopted as a 5-year-old and was now going to return to China, 20 years later, as a 25-year-old.

The Spirit Dream

Morgan had a dream. In the dream, two men were discussing her visa application and then one of the men stamped the application. She received an email within days of the dream that her Chinese visa had been approved.

Stalker

When Morgan was a senior at Texas Tech University, she went on several dates with a police officer from Brownfield, a small town nearby. She decided that their goals and interests were in different directions. Morgan told the policeman that she did not want to date him. She blocked him from social media but found that he had friends following her and reporting to him.

Two years later, I was in my living room one evening and received a call on my cell phone from a Midland P.D. officer about a traffic accident in Midland. The officer asked if I was someone of a different name. I said no. He asked if I was sure.

I said, "Yes, and why are you calling me?" He said that an accident report listed my phone number for a witness of a hit-and-run accident. I told him it must have been an error.

"I'm Dr. Bartlett," I told him.

He continued, "Are you sure you did not witness an accident in Midland?"

"Yes," I told him again.

"That is strange, because your number is in the report as a witness; are you sure?"

"Yes, I'm sure," I affirmed.

"Thank you for taking my call," he said at last, and hung up.

What a bizarre call. I texted the private cell number back, asking for details about why I was called and who called me. Morgan called me the next day from work and said the stalker cop contacted her and said I had called him.

She said the cell number was unknown, so she answered. She was surprised when it was the stalker cop. He told her he had moved to Midland recently and wanted to start dating. She was shaken and told him she had to get back to work and hung up. I told Morgan about the call I received with a bogus story about a car accident.

The next day, my cell phone rang. It was the same cell number the stalker cop had used. I answered. The stalker cop pretended to ask follow-up questions about the accident. I asked if he intended to call me, or Morgan, again. After a long pause, the stalker cop explained that he believed he and I got off on the wrong foot. He said he was calling because Morgan respected my opinion. He said he still had feelings for Morgan, and he was sorry if I didn't like that.

I said he should focus on his career with the new job in Midland. I told him he should take care of the mother of his children and their two kids. After we hung up, I texted him and asked for the case number of the car accident. Several hours later he texted a case number. I asked a friend, Martin Stringer, what he advised. He referred me to the Midland Sheriff. Sheriff Gary Painter called my cell as I drove home from work. I told him what was happening. He said this was a textbook case of stalking. He gave a number for the Assistant Midland Police Chief.

Internal Affairs

I called the Assistant Midland Police Chief and he recommended calling the Internal Affairs officer and gave me the number. The next day, Morgan and I went to the police station to file a report with Internal Affairs. The I.A. officer, Officer Acosta, asked if I still had the text from the stalker cop's personal cell with a case number. Officer Acosta took a screenshot of the text and looked up the case. He told me there was an accident, but my cell number was not in the report and the only witness was a woman. The stalker cop did not work the accident and was not assigned to the case. Officer Acosta advised that I text the stalker cop not to contact Morgan or me again, which I did.

Support and Confirmation

To fund my own participation in the China mission trip, I moonlighted in the ER of the small town of Haskell, Texas, during Thanksgiving. I met some wonderful people there. One gentleman, Ford Cole, was a cotton farmer. Cole had sung in a traveling gospel group for decades. He wanted my number after I told him about my mission trips.

Not long after, I received a letter from Haskell. It included a check for $300 from Ford Cole. We received a text from WMA the next day saying a little over $300 was still needed for the mission. Several weeks later, my son found an unopened letter in our driveway. It must have fallen out of the car by accident days before, as it had tire marks on the envelope. In the second letter, Ford Cole said that he and his wife had driven through their cotton field and it had been unusually productive. They wanted to contribute another $150 to the China mission trip, for Bibles if possible. We forwarded the check to the WMA for Bibles. The next day we received an email from the WMA explaining a need for funds for Bibles. Amazing!

I told my friends in West Texas about the need for Bibles. I found out, weeks later, that during the China trip, thousands of dollars came in for the Bibles. Blane Shuffield, Texas Special Ranger, also sent a check to WMA to support the mission.

In the Sky

On January 3, 2016, Morgan and I flew from Midland to Houston. In Houston, we discovered that Morgan and I were not booked on the same flight over the Atlantic! I watched Morgan board her flight. Later, I sat by an Asian real estate attorney from Houston and her mother, who were flying to Taiwan.

The attorney explained that her father, as a young man, had fought against Mao in the army of Chiang Kai-shek. His army retreated to Taiwan, along with many fellow soldiers. He met her mom in Taiwan and the family still has a home there. I told them about what I had seen Jesus do on the mission trips, and then shared the Best News in the World with them. They had Buddhist beliefs that they were not ready to dismiss. The attorney said she was interested in going on a trip with the WMA. I gave her the website, and my email, if she needed to contact me.

Development

In Germany, Morgan and I boarded the same flight to Sichuan, China. Sichuan was immense. Unlike my trip to China 20 years before, now most of the people were traveling in cars. Twenty years before, flocks of bikes would take off at the city intersections when the light turned green. This time, luxury vehicles were very common and the air was hazy with pollution. I have never had asthma, but I woke up wheezing for the first time. The wheezing resolved spontaneously.

The Underground Church

We went to an underground church service the first day of our mission. Two of our translators, Jackie Lee and Rio Zhang Li (also called Dawn), attended this particular underground church. It was not covert in any way. They had favor in a gated, upscale neighborhood.

The neighborhood community center was available for the underground church services twice a week, without charge. Morgan was quite a sensation. The Chinese were amazed with her story. After she spoke, I presented the Best News in the World. Thirteen people came forward to accept the Lord Jesus and repeated a prayer of salvation after the translator. One was our hired van driver! Many expressed an interest in learning more about the Holy Spirit.

We ate lunch together and then left to go to the townhouse of a church member. In the courtyard, a portable baptismal was set up. The elderly worship leader had members singing hymns they read on their cell phones. The temperature was in the 40s at midday. The warmed water in the trough had steam coming off of it because of the cold temperatures. The constant a cappella singing was the only sound in the neighborhood. Helen Todd, co-founder of the World Missions Alliance, baptized the women who had accepted the Lord. I baptized the two gentlemen who desired baptism. A police officer kept looking in the gate entrance at the crowd singing hymns. The 12 baptismal candidates were wearing choir gowns. The event was very conspicuous. After the baptisms, we prayed with people for health and other needs. Immediate physical healings of back pain and shoulder injuries occurred via prayer, anointing, and acts of faith. Diabetes and insomnia were also issues prayed about. It was a comprehensive church experience with salvations, healings, people being baptized in the Holy Spirit, protection from the police, and favor in the neighborhood.

Seeds

After breakfast, we began our second day in a government Three-Self church, part of the Three-Self Patriotic movement in China, next to our hotel. The government had built the church building in a key location, central to popular businesses and near a university. A Scandinavian architect was hired by the Chinese government to design the building. The Chinese government recruited a Three-Self pastor to run it and gave him the church to use for free. The pastor explained that around 2,000 people attend services each week. He said they often have 30 new visitors each week. He also said 500 people were saved during three meetings over the 2016 Christmas holidays. Another 36 people were baptized at the church during Christmas 2016. Among other petitions, we prayed for clean air for the rest of the trip.

While we were in the church, the front doors were open. Two college students wandered in, curious because the Christmas decorations were still up outside of the church. One student was a Christian and her friend was not. Helen Todd presented the Gospel to them and the young lady prayed to accept Jesus as Lord.

Hot Pot

We took a bus ride to Chongqing, or "Mountain City." During the bus ride one of our translators, Nancy, asked for prayer about her knee pain. She was instantly healed with prayer.

Thirty years ago, the city of Chongqing had 30,000 citizens, but it had since grown to a population of 32 million. That evening, we were brought to a restaurant for "hot pot." Hot pot is a unique dining experience that originated in this city. Two three-foot diameter steel bowls of boiling spices were built into the center of round wooden tables. Plates of raw vegetables and meats were placed on the table. Each individual used chopsticks to put his favorite food items in the boiling pots and then fished them out and ate them once they were cooked. We met several local pastors at the meal.

The Three-Self Church

Pastor Han was one of the pastors of the Three-Self church. He joined us for the remainder of the trip. He was greatly respected nationwide by the government-endorsed Three-Self churches and was a Three-Self church pastor. Our team learned about the Chinese government forming Three-Self churches. The state Three-Self churches involved the principle of Chinese people ministering to Chinese people, Chinese teaching Chinese people, and Chinese funding Chinese churches. It's an effort to safeguard from outside manipulation. Bibles are allowed in churches. It reminded me of the Scripture that the Kingdom of Heaven is like a little leavening that leavened the whole loaf. Allowing just the ingredient of the Bible in the nation would affect the whole nation. The Chinese government cracked the door slightly open for the Gospel to be presented and a massive revival has come to the Chinese people, along with great benefits to the Chinese government.

We visited three state-funded Three-Self churches. The average attendance was 9,000 members each week at one church. That church had five Sunday services. Christian church members who were business-

131

men supported several additional outreach efforts. The efforts included a bookstore that was open to the public with free coffee and snacks. The Moses movie, with actor Ben Kingsley, was playing on a loop, dubbed with Chinese voices on a large-screen TV. A person would wander in from the busy sidewalks to enjoy the central heat and air conditioning that is uncommon downtown. Many visitors would ask spiritual questions and, later, join the congregation. We left Bibles that were donated by the World Missions Alliance. We were also told that the congregation had outreach ministry to the surrounding villages, helping orphans with food and clothing.

The Bride

During the main Sunday morning service, we attended a beautiful church in a prime real estate location, next to a beautiful park in the center of the city. The original church building was built in 1898 by Methodist missionaries and later destroyed by a fire. A larger, more ornate church with beautiful stained-glass windows replaced the original church.

The church inside and out looked like any grand church you would expect to find in Europe or America. A large, robed choir was seated behind the pastor at the front of the church. The congregation sat in large pews under the enormous vaulted ceiling. The present-day city of 30 million was built around the original church in the countryside.

Prior to entering the church, we saw three bridal parties at the park, doing photo shoots. Morgan was thrilled. Prior to the trip, she had been working at a bridal shop helping brides make selections for their weddings. The church had several services every Sunday. Pastor Han was honored to be the guest pastor for the service we attended. The service was orderly; the congregation joined the choir singing hymns from hymnals available on the backs of pews. The pastor gave announcements. His sermon was about the twice-blessed marriage. Pastor Han said marriage is a cooperation made in Heaven. He mentioned the bride of Christ being the church. He also discussed natural marriages from a biblical perspective. Pastor Han quoted Proverbs 31, about the ideal wife.

Twice-Blessed Marriage

He said the twice-blessed marriage is from the Lord. Pastor Han explained that many Jewish people believe there are double blessings on the third day of the week, Tuesday. Therefore, Jews often get married on the third day. He told the congregation that God will give new wine to a blessed marriage, like Jesus gave new wine at the Cana wedding. He quoted John 2, and the story of the first marriage in Genesis. He also quoted Ecclesiastes, that two people are better than one.

I was surprised that Pastor Han used my marriage with Dawn as the grand finale evidence of a twice-blessed marriage from God. He asked Morgan and me to stand up, and he introduced us as a family. We were well received, and the congregation was very gracious and kind. Pastor Han even sang a popular Chinese folk song about weddings. The words were, "When it is wedding time, we will have very good wine, when the wolves come, we will have guns."

During a meal after the church service, Pastor Han spoke favorably about the underground church, calling it "the community church." He said that great improvements have occurred in the relationship between the community churches and the government-run Three-Self churches.

Re-Digging Old Wells of Faith

We toured a Christian museum. There were large photographs and historical artifacts. We heard about churches that were established in 1898 by the Methodist Church. The Methodist Church organization also built hospitals, trained doctors and nurses, and became the hub of the towns. The urban development of the city started around the churches.

God Makes a Way

We were invited to visit a Wednesday night Bible study at one of those Methodist churches. The church bell tower was used by pilots during

World War II to navigate. We were told that this was built in 1894 and was the oldest church property in that part of China. They built the new church building in 1917.

They had two Saturday services and two Sunday services; they regularly had 700 people attend each service. I was allowed to speak for 45 minutes to the congregation. I gave testimonies about my wife and I having a miracle pregnancy and birth child. I also told about the miracle of my adopted son Zachary and how I found his birth mother in the Republic of Georgia, south of Russia. Several other mission team members also spoke. People who were not Chinese citizens had never been allowed to preach or teach at that church before. It was, and is, against the law for that to occur at any church in China.

The Serpent Dream

On January 11, 2017, our last night in China, we had a feast in a fancy restaurant. Classic Chinese dishes swirled slowly on the lazy Susan in the middle of the immense, black, round table. One of our Chinese translators, Nancy Liu, sat by me at the dinner table and said she wanted to tell me her story. She said that her parents already had one child when her mother was pregnant with her.

It was common to abort subsequent pregnancies. Her parents were poor and did hard labor for the government as miners. When her mother went to the abortionist, she told the doctor about a dream she'd had the night before. In the dream she had a snake wrapped around her finger. She shook her hand and was terrified, but she never could get the snake off her finger. The doctor said that was interesting. He told her that her village has a saying, "If you have a dream about a snake wrapped around your finger, your child will be exceptional." The abortionist recommended that she not kill the baby and see what happens with Nancy's life.

Tough Childhood

Shortly after Nancy was born, she was sent to live with grandparents in a remote village until she was six years old. Her grandmother would talk about the heavenly grandfather. It was more of an old wives' tale. She would say, "Don't do the wrong thing, because your heavenly grandfather will see you." There was no relationship expected, or offered, with the heavenly grandfather.

She returned to her parents' factory, which had free government grade schools. Her parents were distant with her. Although she lived in government housing and sometimes they ate together, no affection was ever given. It was not a normal childhood. She attended primary school in that atmosphere. Her father was mean to her on purpose. She would sit next to him and he would say, "Why are you sitting next to me?" She would stand up, and he would say, "Why are you standing?"

It was constant harassment and no love. She started to have suicidal thoughts in secondary school. Despite that, she did well academically and was accepted into a university. The nation of China was changing policies. Women now had more opportunities. Also, free enterprise was developing in China. A person could own a business for 99 years. Nancy met her husband, who was a businessman. She also had businesses. She said that she far exceeded the success of her husband and peers in business. She became prideful. She told me that she and her husband had arguments constantly. She had a successful business, wealth, and a son, but no peace.

She became ill. She often felt weak, dizzy, and short of breath. One day, as she was waiting to cross the street in the busy downtown, she looked at an oncoming bus and the bus driver's face changed to a demon. She screamed in the crowd. She said she saw several other people in the crowd whose faces changed into demons and then returned to normal. No one else saw what she saw.

She went to the doctor and was diagnosed with a heart condition. I surmised that she was diagnosed with pericarditis and placed on corticosteroids such as prednisone. The doctors placed her on the medications, told her that she could never work again, and said she would not live very long. She gained 100 pounds and started having suicidal thoughts again.

She reasoned that this was such a cruel world, she should not only kill herself but kill her son as well. Why would she leave her son in this cruel world by himself? She was desperate. She lit incense and prayed for help to Buddha, the heavenly grandfather she had heard of, and anyone else who was listening. Within the week, she received a Bible tract in the mail, which introduced her to her Heavenly Father. She had never heard that expression before.

She prayed to become a Christian. The Bible tract was mailed from Miami by Chinese Christians who had moved from China to Miami. The tract was part of a random mass mailing. For the first time in her life, she had peace.

Several days later, she was telling her friend about her Heavenly Father. Her friend told her, "I have a book that was given to me. It sounds like it is for you and your God." The friend gave her a bilingual English and Chinese New Testament.

Nancy did not know any other Christians. She had never gone to church. Nancy hid the Bible from friends and family and did not tell them about the Bible or the God of the Bible. She said it was her most precious possession and she kept it secret. She started reading the book of Matthew. She wrote the book of Matthew in English and learned to read and write English as a result. In the process, she reasoned that this Scripture was medicine. She decided that she would "eat" the book of Matthew instead of taking her medications.

She stopped the medicines without asking her doctors. After six months of no medicine, she had lost the excess weight, had her energy and strength restored, and had peace, joy, and patience that she had never experienced before. She and her husband did not argue anymore. Then, one day while she was praying, the thought came to her that she should tell her friends and family about the God of the Bible. She asked her husband for money so she could print more Bibles. He did not hesitate, thankful for the peace that had been in their home for the last six months.

Now, Nancy has helped the World Missions Alliance as a missionary translator for the last 14 years. Her son is a student at the University of Colorado in Denver. Nancy's father became a believer and told Nancy he did not know why he had been so mean to her. He asked her to forgive him and they had a sweet relationship for his remaining years.

Blessings

After the meal, Pastor Han went around the table, speaking a blessing over each member of the mission team. When he got to Morgan his voice broke; he gave an emotional blessing and told her that he would be her Chinese father. Sheryl DeZura prophesied this to me: "God will bless your finances, but not only through your career. There will be support of the ministry. God is going to bless you abundantly to sow into God's Kingdom, and to go when and where He sends you. Because of your obedience in giving of your time, talent, and treasure, even in the harder places, He will bless you and your family." (Deuteronomy 1:11)

Earlier in the day, we went to see the pandas at the Wolong National Nature Reserve. We saw red pandas, and black and white panda bears. It was a great outing. We also toured a prison from the time after World War II—this was on recommendation of the government. We saw the prison cells, torture chamber, and torture equipment. We were told that this was a compound of followers of Chiang Kai-shek, hidden in the jungle. We had many Chinese eyes looking suspiciously at our mission team as we wandered around the oppressive site.

We were also able to do an afternoon of shopping in an ancient shopping market that had been renovated. That was great fun for Morgan and me. Everyone we encountered in the restaurants, hotels, churches, and streets was gracious and hospitable.

We had an uneventful trip back home to Texas.

Reconnecting

Our daughter Morgan reconnected with her crib mate from the orphanage in China via social media. Her crib mate's name was Jessica Wei Wa Abrams. Jessica and Morgan were adopted from China at the same time; while Morgan grew up in Texas with my wife and I, Jessica was raised in New York by a Jewish, single mother who was a lawyer. After 20 years, Morgan and Jessica found each other on Facebook and started keeping up with each other's lives.

In the summer of 2016, we raised a litter of registered German Shepherds. Morgan helped me take care of the mother while she was delivering the puppies. Morgan posted on Facebook that the German Shepherd puppies were for sale. Jessica's mother heard about the German Shepherd puppies and flew down from New York with Jessica's sister. They bought one of our puppies and flew back to New York. In October of 2016, Jessica contacted Morgan saying that she was in Austin doing some work for FEMA. She wanted to drive up to our house from Austin to visit. It had been 20 years since Morgan had last seen Jessica Wei Wa.

Jessica arrived at our house on October 6, 2017, a Friday, at around 11 p.m. As soon as she got off work from Austin, she drove six hours straight to our house. When she walked in the front door, she was literally shaking, she was so excited. She sat on the couch next to Morgan and Dawn. For the first 10 minutes or so, we enjoyed random small talk. It was clear, however, that Jessica was very excited and wide awake. Prior to Jessica's arrival, Morgan had told me that Jessica's mother, Florence, did not want us to speak with her about religion. Florence is an Orthodox Jew and told Morgan that Jessica had turned away from religion, and Florence did not want us to make Jessica more turned off by religion.

After we had talked for 10 minutes I felt compelled to tell Jessica the Best News in the World. I told Jessica that, obviously, I am a man of science since I'm a medical doctor. I told her I know she is a woman of science, since she does cartography for FEMA to help rescue people during disasters.

I said that, by definition, a scientific fact must be both observable and reproducible. We all have experienced things that go beyond the understanding of science, which can only be explained by the spiritual or the supernatural. The spiritual experiences are no less real than the scientific experiences. When I told her about the Messiah, Jesus Christ, she said she was interested in accepting Him as her savior. So, we led Jessica in a prayer of salvation that night.

Fun Together

The next day, Morgan and Jessica went shopping together and had a great day. They bought matching outfits and ate out together, really enjoying the time and the chance to talk. The following morning, October 8, 2017, Jessica decided to go to church with us at Midland Cornerstone Church. That is the church of Ryan Hall, who had been dating Morgan. Ryan had gone through a year of schooling in Christian religion at Cornerstone church. That morning service included the graduation ceremony for his class.

Ryan told my wife and me that he was going to propose to Morgan during the service. Morgan knew about the graduation ceremony but had no clue about the proposal. The large church was packed with extra seats in the aisles and many people were taking pictures and videoing with their phones. The keynote speaker spoke about God and then a commencement ceremony began.

All of the graduates marched across the stage in their caps and gowns to receive their diplomas, shake hands, and pose for pictures. During the ceremony, Morgan had slipped to the front of the stage to take some pictures of Ryan as he was graduating; she had no idea what was about to happen. When it was Ryan's turn to come to the stage, the pastor, Bill Foster, stopped the ceremony and gave Ryan the microphone. Ryan asked Morgan to join him up on the stage.

Morgan came up on the stage and Ryan got on his knee and asked her to marry him, right there in front of the entire congregation and God Himself. There was a surprisingly long pause, causing all to wonder how she might answer. Later, Morgan explained that her ears started to hiss and the room became fuzzy. She saw his lips moving, but she couldn't hear him. She felt like she was going to pass out. But, she decided that he probably asked her to marry him, so she said yes. The room erupted in celebration.

Jessica had not been a part of our life for 20 years, and yet she had suddenly felt a strong and unexplainable urge to leave work in Austin and drive non-stop to our house on the same weekend that Morgan became engaged to be married. Morgan asked Jessica to be a bridesmaid. They spent that Sunday afternoon visiting friends of mine at the radio and TV stations, as well as other friends in Midland and Odessa.

A Blessed Union

On April 14, 2018, Ryan Hall and Morgan Bartlett were married. Jessica Abrams was one of the bridesmaids and the wedding was a wonderful celebration. Parker Heights Church in Odessa was packed. Jessica flew in from New York the day before the ceremony and spent the weekend with our family. It seemed like she had always been a member of our family.

During the wedding ceremony, in front of the congregation and guests, I said that we knew Ryan was a special person when he was dating Morgan. I spoke about when Morgan and I returned to China, in January 2017. Ryan and Morgan were already dating at the time of that trip. We should have known that this marriage would happen when Morgan saw all those bridal parties having photo shoots in front of the church where Pastor Han preached about the twice-blessed marriage.

There were so many signs that Ryan was meant to be a part of our family. Back in June of 2017, Morgan and Ryan were dating. Morgan, Dawn, and Grant saw both Ryan and me off at the Midland Airport.

Ryan was headed to Thailand with a group on a mission trip lead by Pastor Bill Foster at the same time as I was headed off to Lebanon for my missions work. It was satisfying to see the young man who was dating my daughter go help people in Thailand.

After Ryan and Morgan's honeymoon in Greece and Italy, Morgan returned complaining of nausea. She was pregnant. Ryan had repeated raises and promotions at work. He was given a company pickup as a job benefit. Ryan's company added a new benefit that their employees would get a two-month paid paternity leave to bond with their infants. Nathaniel was born on January 15, 2019. The paid paternity leave benefit was stopped a year after their baby was born.

Looking back, it's clear that the Lord had plans for a twice-blessed marriage for an "unwanted" Chinese orphan girl. Satan tried to derail these plans but the Lord prevailed! Romans 8:28 (TLB) says, "And we know that all that happens to us is working for our good if we love God and are fitting into His plans."

Jeremiah 29:11 NIV:

"For I know the plans I have for you," declares the Lord, "plans to prosper you and not harm you, plans to give you hope and a future."

Government Persecutes Christians

It has always been illegal in Communist China to tell anyone under 18 years old about Jesus. Parents risk prison if they tell their own children in the privacy of their home about God. Teachers risk prison if they mention any religion to children. I never saw a youth at any of the gatherings on our trip. After our trip, Chinese President Xi started a systematic persecution of Christians. Church leaders are imprisoned and churches demolished by the government for crossing this legal line. Face recognition software is used in conjunction with CCTV in churches in China for enforcement. The underground home church movement exists due to this issue and other government oppression. Bob Fu of ChinaAid helps rescue tortured, imprisoned, and hunted Christians out of China. For more information, contact ChinaAid.org. Bob Fu is author of *God's Double Agent: The True Story of a Chinese Christian's Fight for Freedom,* available on Amazon (Baker Books, 2013).

Police and military resources have been diverted from persecuting Christians in China because of plagues. In 2019, African swine fever killed a third of the pigs in China. Pork is the main protein source for Asia. The coronavirus (COVID-19) also diverted government resources from persecuting the Chinese Christians. The economy of the atheist government has been damaged. I expect other plagues parallel to Egypt's experience when God said, "Let my people go!"

Photos Taken in China

Morgan and 30 million people.

30 million people in China, on the move.

China state seminary.

Underground baptism in China.

Morgan and Dr. Bartlett at the Panda Scientific Discovery Center.

Baby panda at the panda reserve.

Morgan and Jessica.

Morgan gets engaged.

China 2017.

CHAPTER 5

Cannibals

"For we wrestle not against flesh and blood, but against principalities, against powers, against the rulers of the darkness of this
world, against spiritual wickedness in high places."
—Ephesians 6:12 KJV

"And having spoiled principalities and powers, he made a
shew of them openly, triumphing over them in it."
—Colossians 2:15 KJV

Traveling in Comfort

A friend of mine is a family nurse practitioner named Deanna Moore.
She has said many times that she would like to go on a medical mission
to Ethiopia, however she was concerned she might see needs beyond
her abilities. De has excellent medical skills and knowledge; I knew she
would be a tremendous asset on a medical mission. She said she would
like to go on a mission with me before she became the solo medical
provider on a trip.

February 2017

We flew from Houston to Frankfurt. I'm not usually one of those people
who get to spread out onto other seats and sleep during international

flights. I've noticed on other international trips that there are professional travelers who clearly know how to do things. Always the first on board, they find a bunch of empty seats in a row and, before you know it, they've got their sleeping clothes on and are collapsed across the seats, out for the night.

This time, shortly after takeoff, I was pleased to find an empty row of seats. The flight attendant gave me a nice blanket and I was able to sleep for the majority of the trip. I landed in Germany feeling like I was already having a great trip. My plane experience was quite enjoyable, with the good sleep and quality movie selection. As a bonus, I wasn't ill this time, unlike so many previous mission trips. As I left the plane, I found De and we raced through the Frankfurt Airport to our gate.

Frankfurt

We had to run to get to the gate on time due to the short layover. We were ready for the next leg of our trip from Frankfurt, Germany to Addis Ababa, Ethiopia. I let Deanna go through first since she's the lady. She showed her passport and ticket, stepping through without incident. When I reached for my passport in my inside coat pocket, I found it missing. I searched all my pockets and realized it must have fallen out when I wadded my coat up for a pillow on the last plane. I was panicking. I told the lady at the gate that it must have fallen out of my pocket when I wadded up my coat for a pillow while I slept on the flight. She was understanding of my plight and made a call. She told me the captain of my last plane said they have my passport and will try to get it to me. I couldn't go back through the gates and checkpoints to the plane, due to security.

I went over to the nearest customer service counter and waited. I was anxious and kept asking for updates. Time was ticking by fast. I studied every passerby. "Could it be him? He looks official. He kept walking past the gate. She is wearing a uniform. No, not her." Time kept slipping by and still nobody showed up with my passport. They supposedly had someone coming to deliver it, but I was becoming increasingly doubtful. At five minutes before the plane was to depart, it became obvious that I was going to have to find another flight.

I went to the nearest counter where I could schedule a new flight from Germany to Ethiopia only to discover that the next available flight was 12 hours later! I was so disappointed that I was going to have to wait half a day in Frankfurt and delay my work in Ethiopia. Everything had seemed to be going so well! I bought my new ticket for an extra $400. After I finally recovered my passport, the flight agent recommended I take the train from the airport into Frankfurt and look around. I initially thought it seemed too risky, since things had already gotten somewhat derailed, but I eventually decided to give it a try. I found the right train and headed toward Frankfurt.

I nearly panicked while I was on the train. The overhead voice was announcing the stops in German. The maps and signs were in German only. The nearby conversations were all in German. I don't speak any German. I realized in that moment, at least in part, what a refugee might feel like arriving in a new country where they don't speak the language. It was very unnerving. I found several people on the train who spoke broken English and they helped me get off at the right stop. I walked around downtown Frankfurt, staying near the train stop. I found a clothing store where I bought a few gifts for my family. I decided I wasn't going to risk further delays, so I headed back to the airport and spent my remaining hours simply waiting.

Meeting by God's Hand

On the plane from Frankfurt to Ethiopia I sat in the middle aisle. There was an African lady who sat in my row and we had empty seats between us. I started talking to her. At first she responded cautiously, but after we started talking more it became clear that she was a Christian. Her name was Josianne Etoile Duseigneur, from Cameroon, Africa. We basically had a six-hour church service in the air! We fervently and unabashedly prayed together for each other's families. The Holy Spirit was speaking prophetic words out of her mouth to me, and out of my mouth to her.

At times I was aware that people in other seats would turn and look at us. I imagine it was bizarre that this American, speaking West Texas slang, and an African with a French accent, who had nothing apparent in common, were getting along so well. We were talking animatedly together, holding hands with closed eyes as we prayed for each other's families. At one point in the middle of the flight, I told her I felt like the Lord was saying that she was the Joyce Meyer of Africa. She asked me who Joyce Meyer was. Other people had prophesied to her that she was the Joyce Meyer of Africa, but she had no idea who Joyce Meyer was. I explained to her that Joyce Meyer is a lady who has an anointing to teach and she has chosen wisely to teach other women. As a woman teaching other women, she has been extremely successful. She teaches, writes books, and takes mission trips to other countries. Josianne was very encouraged.

Family Stories

During the flight, she asked about my family. I told her the story of my seven children. I explained that the first six were adopted. I told her that three of my children are from the countries China, Latvia, and the Republic of Georgia. I told her how thankful my wife and I are for every child. I shared how we did not adopt a whole bunch of kids in one big group, but that each adoption was its own story of God's miracles. I told her how, after 20 years of being married, my wife turned 40. My wife told me she was not getting any younger and if she was ever going to get pregnant it needed to happen soon. I wisely didn't respond. I told Josianne that I am a doctor and am well aware of how these things happen.

It had been specifically prophesied to us that we would have a birth child. For 20 years, we waited for our miracle son, but it had not happened yet. I told Josianne that I prayed quietly, "Lord, I know what you do for one, you can do for another. Isaac and Rebecca were married for 20 years, and Rebecca had been called barren. You gave them the miracle pregnancy with twins. I pray you would do that for Dawn." While I was happy with our six children, I knew that it was a real issue

CANNIBALS

for my wife. In Proverbs, it says that four things are never satisfied. One of those is the barren womb.

I understood that women are wired differently than men. My wife desired to have the experience of a birth child, although she loved all our children. For her, I prayed that God would give us a birth child. Shortly after that prayer, she started feeling dizzy and lightheaded. She became concerned and insisted that I order a CAT scan for her.

The radiologist told me the CAT scan was normal. I called my wife and told her I'd just talked to the radiologist. She stopped me and said that before I tell her anything else, she wanted to tell me what just happened. She went out to her car after the CAT scan and turned on the radio. A lady on the radio was telling her story. Doctors thought she had a tumor. They ordered a CAT scan and found out she was pregnant. Dawn asked if I thought that could happen to her. I said, well, you don't have a tumor. We met and ate lunch. A couple of days later, she called me into the bathroom to show me a pregnancy test strip with two pink lines on it. She asked me what that meant. I told her, "That means you're pregnant."

Dawn didn't want to be disappointed again because she's been disappointed every month for 20 years. She told me to find a pregnancy test that had the word "pregnant" printed on it. I went to the neighborhood dollar store in our small Texas town. Thank God they had a pregnancy test that had the word "pregnant" on it. I brought the test back and, sure enough, the word "pregnant" showed up on the test strip. Naturally, there was a big celebration.

After I finished telling the story to Josianne, she said she felt humbled. She told me she was currently pregnant with her fifth child. She had felt like this pregnancy was a burden. She told me it had cost a lot, and had been a lot of work, to raise the four children she already had. When she found out she was pregnant again, it was not expected. She hadn't been happy about it and was actually resenting the pregnancy. Josianne said that, after hearing my story, she knew she had to repent.

153

She realized she had the wrong attitude and decided to become thankful for the pregnancy.

Family History

I told her more stories about my family of miracles. She told me miracles from her family. Toward the end of the flight, she felt comfortable enough to tell me a very sensitive family story. Josianne explained that in Cameroon, the people are tribal. Everything there revolves around tribes. Her family tribe was wicked in witchcraft. She said when her grandfather was a little boy, their tribe would steal people from other tribes and eat them. In response, the other tribes banded together and wiped out all the adults of her family's tribe. Her grandfather was a little child at that time, so they let him live with the other children because they weren't a threat. As time went by her grandfather got pulled back into witchcraft by witches from other tribes.

Josianne's grandfather ended up having a total of nine children. One of those was Josianne's father. Seven of the nine children of her grandfather were eaten by witches as little children. Josianne's aunt was her father's surviving sibling. The aunt was named after the witches that had eaten her siblings. I thought about how powerful a name is. From Genesis to Revelation, the Bible highlights the importance of a person's name. I felt terrible for this poor little girl, named after the witches who ate her siblings. Josianne said that, when her grandmother became pregnant with her father, her grandmother ran to the city and hid so the child would not be killed.

Her father grew up in the city, protected. When he was 18 he acted like many 18-year-old boys do: stupidly. He decided to go back to the village where his ancestors were from and stayed there until after dark. He was captured in the night and put through rituals and ceremonies, and placed in a coffin. She said they ate part of her father's body and then he lost his mind. I wondered if he became possessed. Josianne said that when she was born, her father did a ceremony to dedicate her to Satan. When she was a little girl, she would see demons and other things that no one else could see. She thought she was going crazy.

Finding Christ

There was an older, Christian lady in the village who told Josianne about Jesus and led Josianne to Christ. Josianne clung to Christ. She was hungry to learn anything she could from the Bible. She learned anything she could from this Christian lady. They would often pray. She told the lady she thought she might lose her mind. In desperation, she clung to Christianity and her relationship with Christ. In time, she found that there was one Christian college and seminary in Cameroon, and she wanted to go there. Josianne gave it her all; she worked hard and she got herself into the college. She told me how thankful she was for this Christian college.

The college did not have a big reputation at the time, but it was quite academic on many levels. Josianne said she used her knack for promotion and helped the college start to flourish. The Lord gave her a prophecy, which she shared with the headmaster of the college. He laughed at her and thought it was ridiculous. After it came to pass, he started to seek her out to hear from the Lord even though she was just a lowly freshman. Josianne did her best, studied hard, and graduated from this Christian college and seminary.

The headmaster asked her at one point why witches can't stand to be around her. He said witches told him they couldn't stand to be near her because they saw fire in her eyes. Josianne still had the gift of seeing things in the spirit world. She could see demons and angels, and she had a gift of prophecy. She confided that her heart's desire was to become a pastor, though as a woman she didn't feel she should do that. I told her that made perfect sense to me, with the prophecy I'd delivered to her earlier. She could be a pastor and teacher of women. She could have a tremendous ministry and, if she turns the hearts of the women to the Lord, that will change families. She would be ministering indirectly to men and children too. I told her I believe she has a tremendous calling on her life. Josianne was greatly encouraged.

Seeing Demons

Josianne told me another fascinating story about her family on the flight from Germany to Ethiopia. She explained that her husband had gotten a contract to work in Germany. She was able to travel with him from Cameroon and live in Germany for a while because of his employment. She told me how they started attending a very conservative Lutheran church in Germany. The people were lovely. She came into the service one day and saw a young lady speaking to the pastor, at the front of the church before the service started. Josianne saw that the lady had demons. Josianne walked up to the front and told the lady, the pastor, and the assistant pastor, that this lady had demons and should be kept away from the children. The pastor laughed at Josianne, dismissed her, and apologized to the lady.

Several days later, Josianne got a phone call from the pastor saying she wouldn't believe what just happened. The pastor went on to tell Josianne that the woman she had accused of having demons was in charge of the church's children's ministry. Well, the pastor's oldest daughter had a birthday and the lady with the demon in her had given a gift, to both his teenage daughter and his younger daughter, who was about five years old. It turned out the presents got confused. Witnessed by the pastor, the two sisters opened the gifts from this lady and found it full of pornography and sex toys. The pastor was shocked. The pastor called Josianne to tell her there was no doubt she had been correct.

Ethiopia

After we landed at the airport in Ethiopia, Josianne and I took a picture of us together to commemorate the meeting. She caught a connecting flight to Cameroon. I was picked up by local pastors and taken to the rest of the mission team. I entered the airport with the rest of the passengers. I found my checked duffel bag on the baggage carousel and made my way to a security check. The airport was an open structure with chipped and missing tiles, yellowed paint on the walls, and the smell of body odor. I retrieved my orange duffel bag from the baggage carousel and walked toward the security agent. I noticed a black lady in colorful, stylish clothes who was obviously frustrated with the teenage female agent rifling through her large suitcase. Clothing and personal belongings were falling from the counter onto the filthy floor.

The woman was muttering under her breath and shaking her head, clearly displeased. Even from a distance, it was clear the agent was enjoying herself. She would share a smirk and sideways glance with the four other teenage agents in uniform as they would amble past or lounge at the end of the terminal. I was asked to open my duffel. Bundles of packaged pills in white plastic rolls were all that could be seen. The teenage boy agent's eyes widened like he had hit the mother lode. He turned to me with a squinting grimace and pointed to seats next to the frustrated woman who was gathering underwear from the floor. In short order, I had four teenage agents swarming around my duffel, excitedly speaking Ethiopian and gesturing my direction from time to time.

Chuck Todd appeared with the local pastor to pick me up. I waved them over. They joined me on the bench and I explained what was happening. The teenager in charge grilled me. I explained that we are a Christian organization that provides free medical care to the poor around the world. We are treated with respect and welcomed in nation after nation. From his jewelry, scowl, and line of questioning, he was clearly Muslim and did not approve. Hours later, after presenting passports, copies of licenses and certificates, and a manifest of the medication, we were released with our tourist visas but without the duffel.

Fortunately, Deanna Moore had made it through with the other duffel of medicine earlier. Half of the meds were available for the first three days of clinics, which we performed on the grounds of the Messianic Jewish Synagogue. I returned to the airport on the fourth day of the trip for a full day of classic extortion shakedown by the airport agents. This led to paying an extra $400 for the release of the medicine, which was used for the remainder of the trip.

Everything in Ethiopia seemed to be covered with dust. The classic third-world wafts of sewer vapor would catch you by surprise as you traveled the city past the poor, hollow-faced people who lived on the streets. New six-story buildings were being constructed with concrete blocks. The scaffolding surrounding the walls was made of bamboo and sticks tied together for six stories of death-defying adventure. I noticed there weren't any middle-aged or older men present on the sites. I'm certain the life expectancy is short in that vocation.

The church was in the city proper. Every day, an iron gate was unlocked by two emaciated elderly men attending the gate as "guards" who let us in the church grounds. There was nothing to steal, even if someone broke in with that intent. The congregation was being charged a heavy rent from a Muslim property owner. They had recently received notice that the property was for sale and they would have to vacate. The Rabbi said they had no plan yet.

The Ethiopian Jews are treated as outcasts by their Muslim and Orthodox neighbors. They are the poorest of society. Rabbi Mekassa was raised in an Ethiopian Jewish family. When he accepted Jesus (Yeshua) as his Messiah, his family and the Jewish community disowned him. His wife and children were cut off from relatives. Many of the members of the local Jewish congregation slept on pieces of cardboard on the sidewalks at night. We had several night services that we attended with the local congregation. The attendees were clean but had very worn clothing. They were quick to smile, with hope in their eyes. During the services, they sang loudly with zeal and prayed with fervor. They had no earthly possessions, yet they exuded hope, peace, and love. The rabbi explained that many were hungry but they would still give the little scraps of change they acquired from odd jobs to the church so the poorest could eat.

CANNIBALS

Luke 14:26-35 NIV:

"If anyone comes to me and does not hate father and mother, wife and children, brothers and sisters—yes, even their own life—such a person cannot be my disciple. And whoever does not carry their cross and follow me cannot be my disciple.

"Suppose one of you wants to build a tower. Won't you first sit down and estimate the cost to see if you have enough money to complete it? For if you lay the foundation and are not able to finish it, everyone who sees it will ridicule you, saying, 'This person began to build and wasn't able to finish.'

"Or suppose a king is about to go to war against another king. Won't he first sit down and consider whether he is able with ten thousand men to oppose the one coming against him with twenty thousand? If he is not able, he will send a delegation while the other is still a long way off and will ask for terms of peace. In the same way, those of you who do not give up everything you have cannot be my disciples.

"Salt is good, but if it loses its saltiness, how can it be made salty again? It is fit neither for the soil nor for the manure pile; it is thrown out.

"Whoever has ears to hear, let them hear."

Grieving

During one evening service, the rabbi called a 12-year-old girl forward to be ministered to. He explained that her father had died recently. The congregation prayed and sang over her while she grieved. She fell to her knees, crying, and pounded the floor with her fists. She filled the synagogue with heart-wrenching wailing and sobs while the congregation continued to pray and sing over her for some time. When it was over, she quietly got up and returned to her seat in the middle of the congregation. The service continued like nothing had ever happened. She appeared peaceful and joyful when she left after the service with several friends.

Medical Clinics in Tents

Two tents were erected on the property of the synagogue: the nurse and the nurse practitioner used one tent while I used the second tent for my medical clinic. At times, the rabbi would join me as an interpreter. Other times, local congregation members translated for me. A Muslim mother and her two children prayed, in unison, to accept Jesus as their Savior. Another Muslim woman carried her brain-damaged 5-year-old stepdaughter to the clinic. We looked at the CAT scan pictures, medical records, and reports of severe damage. We prayed for both of them. The mother prayed to accept Yeshua (Jesus) as her Savior.

The rabbi was thrilled to translate for me, as many Muslims were presented with the Good News and accepted the Lord. In total, 17 souls prayed to accept Yeshua (Jesus) as their Savior during the medical clinics. Ten of those people later began attending the foundation classes offered at the congregation.

Bar Mitzvah

Rabbi Mekasha's oldest son, who had turned 13 years old, was scheduled to have his Bar Mitzvah while we were on the mission. That was my first Bar Mitzvah attendance, and I was curious about the different traditions. I noticed the rabbi's wife lighting candles in front of the congregation as everyone prayed. She was on her knees and wearing a prayer shawl, praying with her arms outstretched. She gathered all the children in front of her and covered them with the shawl while she prayed. It was a literal picture of Psalms 91:1-4. It also struck me as a visual of how Christ wanted to gather the Jews, like a mother hen gathers her chicks. (Matthew 23:37, Luke 13:34)

Moving in Unison

As the service began, the Rabbi Mekasha asked several of the men in our group if they would like to blow the shofar (an ancient musical horn used for Jewish religious purposes). Three declined before he offered it to me. I said yes. He told me that, at a set time, we would both blow the shofars. He had read in Numbers 10 that the people of God would blow the shofar once to gather the people of God and a second time to signal the people of God to move out. He gave me a long shofar while he blew a short shofar. After the second blowing of the shofars, the congregation broke out in worship, praise, and thanksgiving! Not a single soul or voice was silent in the jubilee.

Manhood

The rabbi's son came forward with the children from the congregation. They sang some classic Jewish songs in Hebrew. Then the rabbi came forward and spoke a blessing over his son. He took the cap off of his own head and placed it on his son's. The rabbi's wife brought out a large cake, with sparklers on top, and presented it to their son. The rabbi even handed him cash during the ceremony. The WMA team gave the son an envelope of money as well. Later, during the ceremony, he respectfully told Chuck, "Thank you, sir, for the gift. I have decided to give it to the synagogue." Tears ran down his father's cheeks. Leanora, a mission team member, was led to give him more money. She explained that he had sown into the Kingdom of God and he reaped a harvest for that decision. The boy was speechless and sat by his mom, silently weeping in her arms. It was a holy and precious moment in God's presence.

Each Member Brought Something

Leanora brought the elements of communion. The year prior, I had experienced the power of communion on the mission field in Egypt. I appreciated the importance of communion more after that mission. There were many blessings. WMA staffer Chantel gave attentive care to the team. Billy, a former Green Beret, gave a tearful testimony and blessing to the congregation. Morgan McCasland brought his teenaged daughter Anna on the trip. Anna brought an assortment of fingernail polish and made many local ladies feel special. Deanna, the nurse practitioner, made the generous sacrifice of talent, time, and money for the medical clinic to happen on this trip. Deanna's and her husband, Ken's, generosity made the medical clinic possible. Madeleine provided constant coverage with prayers. Errol Koshman, the seasoned ICU nurse, helped with pharmacy needs and the clinic. Errol gave his moving testimony of spiritual growth. Veteran nurse Toni worked beside me on the last clinic day, which was very fruitful. Patricia prayed and blessed the congregation with great zeal. The Skaggs family donated the medicine. Blane Shuffield's generosity and prayers from Texas blessed the medical mission. Each member was vital!

Our Last Night

On the last day of our mission trip, we were eating dinner at a restaurant with Rabbi Mekasha Kassa, to celebrate our time in Ethiopia. Although he did not know about my conversation with Josianne, he shared a story about a similar experience he'd had. He told us about a young Ethiopian man, who had been employed in Germany and had joined his congregation one evening for a service. At the very beginning of the service, he noticed that this young man pulled out a pair of handcuffs and put them on himself. The rabbi went over to the young man and discreetly asked what he was doing. The young man told the rabbi that he sometimes loses control and didn't want to hurt anybody during the service. He bought the handcuffs and wore them so he couldn't hurt anyone. The rabbi told him it didn't need to be that way, and he prayed for the young man, just a 30 second prayer. He took the handcuffs off and threw them away. Nothing inappropriate happened during the service and he never saw that young man again.

Several months later, the rabbi received a phone call from Germany. It was the pastors of a Lutheran church in Germany. They said they know the young man who came to the rabbi's church. They told the rabbi about the huge change they had seen in the young man's life since receiving the rabbi's prayers. The pastors said they wanted to pay his way to come speak at their church in Germany. At first he wasn't sure if this was a legitimate phone call, but he ended up flying to Germany to speak at a huge Lutheran church. The rabbi shared with me how, when he was standing in front of the congregation, before he started speaking, the Lord told him something and he told it to the congregation.

The Lord told him there were five people in that church building who were possessed with demons. Immediately, those five people had obvious manifestations of demon possession and the whole church service went crazy. He told me that this service was normally very conservative and was supposed to last for one hour; that service lasted for five hours and all five of those people were delivered from the demons and put back in their right minds. An assistant pastor was one of the five that manifested demon possession and was delivered.

By the end of the service, that assistant pastor was in front of the church yelling, "Hallelujah! Praise the Lord, He set me free!"

The rabbi said he stayed there for several days. The congregation allowed the assistant pastor to keep his position and they treated him with compassion.

I saw a familiar thread in the rabbi's story and knew it was not by accident that the Lord let me hear both of these stories: Josianne telling about going to a Lutheran church in Germany where she had the insight and discernment to identify demon possession, and another story of the same kind from a totally unrelated person. The Lord had me hear both of these stories within 10 days.

Letters From Abroad

After returning from my mission trip to Ethiopia, I started receiving letters from abroad. An email from Rabbi Mekasha Kassa read, "Shalom, my dear brother Dr. Richard, I believe you arrived safely and found your great family in peace. Thank you so much for your great love and effort to help our community. Your love impacted many people here. People are telling me a lot. There were 17 people saved, 10 of whom are attending our foundation class regularly. Sincerely, Your Brother, Rabbi Mekasha"

On May 14, 2017, I received another email from Rabbi Mekasha Kassa that read, "Glory and honor to the one who makes the difference.

My wife was the only survivor of a terrible accident. She is recovering quickly, thank you, Doctor." He explained in other emails that his wife had been driving their minivan, which had been donated to him. I remember they had been so proud of that minivan when I visited. Then she was in a terrible accident and lost her daughter as well as the minivan. The rabbi's wife was suffering through the loss and continuing back pain since the accident. Still, in each email he was only thankful and never complaining.

In May of 2017, Josianne sent an email. She wrote, "Shalom Richard, I hope that you're fine. First of all, I want to apologize about my silence. I was so sick here and near death, but God didn't permit it."

A second email came on July 4, 2017: " . . . I struggle for the moment to know that God is with me. I'm struggling for a moment, but you know that God is with me. Best regards to your family and remain in God's peace."

I emailed Josianne back: "Excited to hear from you! I had to show my relatives your picture on my phone and tell them your story. The Joyce Meyer of Cameroon! Be encouraged in Jesus' name. Jesus loves you very much. His angels are ministering spirits sent to meet your needs now because you are an heir of salvation. I just returned from a mission trip to Lebanon and Jesus is on the move. Many Muslims are having visits from Jesus and a huge harvest of souls is being brought to abundant life. Be encouraged. Jesus sees you too. Let me know what is happening in your family. Grace and peace, Richard."

On July 7, 2017, I received a return email from Josianne: "My precious brother in Christ Richard, I was really happy to read your email and your answer proved to me that I can count on you. So many wonderful miracles are happening here. I have so many things to tell you, but in the moment, I am so tired. . . . God bless you and my best regards for your family."

On July 8, I wrote to Josianne and said, "I have told all my friends and family about you and your wonderful family. I am always excited to get news from you. Thanks for your prayers. Record yourself telling reports of what the Lord is doing or write it down. Blessings, Richard."

On August 9, 2017, I received another email that read, "My dear, beloved brother Richard. The moment is so near, and I didn't want to worry you the entire pregnancy, but I have a sickness which is a little rare, called symphysis. Do you know something about it? I have been having difficulty walking, and sometimes I have been paralyzed during the pregnancy, so I need a miracle of God. . . . God bless you and I hope that the next message will be good news."

So on August 9, 2017, I sent an email that said, "Dear sister Josianne Etoile, I'm praying now and will ask others to join in prayer for you. I agree with you that nothing is impossible for the Lord, who loves you. His word doesn't return void, and I am praying his word for you. First Peter 2:24, and Psalms 103. Jeremiah 29:11. Acts 16:31. Mark 16:17-18. No weapon formed against Etoile or her family shall prosper. And every word that rises up against them, in judgment is condemned and proved wrong, because that is your heritage as a servant of the Lord, and your righteousness is of Me, says the Lord."

On August 18, 2017, I received an email from Josianne: "Thank you, my dear, beloved brother, for your support. I am really grateful to have met you through God's hand. Please, I have something important to share with you. Would you be interested in becoming the spiritual father or godfather of my son?"

September 22, 2017, I received a wonderful message from Josianne that read: "Excuse me because the good news had to wait more than three weeks. Our little David-Moses was born the 27th of August through a C-section surgery . . ."

I emailed her that I would be glad to be a godfather for little David-Moses, the baby she was pregnant with on our flight together.

In August 2018, I showed up for duty at the ER in Odessa, Texas. The man who is a lab consultant was in to make sure all was in order in the lab for an expected state inspection. He introduced himself to me. Arnaud Nangne lived in Cameroon until he was 13 years old. His grandfather was king of his tribe. The grandfather sent daughters to surrounding kings to ensure peace with surrounding tribes. Arnaud was related to kings of three tribes in Cameroon! He pulled up the websites of the tribes. I saw his cousin, who is the current king of his tribe. One of the current kings on the other tribes had a carved head on his back facing forward. I discerned witchcraft. I asked Arnaud, "What is that?" He shook his head and said, "I don't know."

I told Arnaud about Josianne's tribe having cannibalism and witchcraft in their past. He started laughing and mocking me. He googled cannibalism in Cameroon and the laughter stopped. He is from the industrialized capital of west Cameroon. The internet had articles of cannibal tribes in east Cameroon. Arnaud said Cameroon has over 200 tribes, each with their own dialect. Arnaud is Catholic because the French controlled Cameroon for decades and brought the Catholic culture and the French language with them. Arnaud moved with his family to France at 13 years old. While in France, Arnaud went to college and got married to a Cameroon lady of the same tribe. His father arranged the marriage. Arnaud currently lives in Houston and said there is a large Cameroon population in Houston. Maybe I will go to Cameroon . . . to be continued!

On the Front Lines

A friend, Getaneh Getaneh, has a ministry named Watch and Pray. He was tortured by Communist Muslims in his birth nation of Ethiopia for sharing the Good News with Muslims. Getaneh prayed for a dead child in Somalia who was raised from the dead. For more info contact WatchandPrayMinistries.org.

Photos Taken in Ethiopia

Rabbi Mekasa and patient at tent.

Josianne and Dr. Bartlett at Addis Ababa Airport.

Statue honoring the King of Kings in Ethiopia.

Addis Ababa.

Construction scaffolding in Addis Ababa.

Street vendors in Addis Ababa.

Street vendors in Addis Ababa.

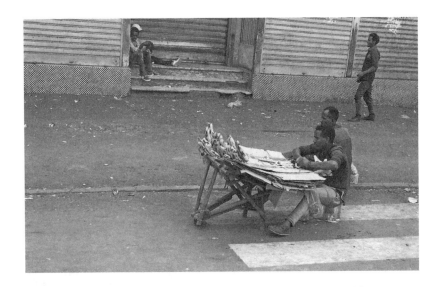

Street vendors in Addis Ababa.

CHAPTER 6

King Jesus Saves Despite Ramadan

For God so loved the world, that he gave his only begotten Son, that whosoever believeth in him should not perish, but have everlasting life. For God sent not his Son into the world to condemn the world; but that the world through him might be saved.

—John 3:16-17 NKJV

Lebanon in the News – The Prelude

On April 25, 2017, an article was on *BBC News* titled, "Meeting an Organ Trafficker who Preys on Syrian Refugees" by Alex Forsyth. In the article, the author meets a man who preys on refugees in Lebanon. A group whose business was selling organs for transplantation had contacted the gentleman. The man admitted to preying on the refugees. He said that the law in Lebanon restricts the refugees from getting jobs or obtaining aid, which means they are trapped. They end up with mounting debt. They've come from utter disaster in Syria or Iraq, and they are looking for any way to pay their bills.

One story told in the article was that of a 17-year-old refugee from Syria. The young man's father and brothers had been murdered in Syria. He'd been living in Lebanon as a refugee for three years, since he was 14. Since the death of his father, he had been helping take care of his mother and five sisters. Mounting debt with no hope of future income was crushing them. The organ trafficker found this young boy and made a deal to buy his right kidney for $8,000. As with all his other victims, he blindfolded this young man and drove him to an abandoned house that had been turned into a makeshift operating room. His kidney was taken out. He was blindfolded again, taken to a different location, and watched for three days. The stitches were removed, and he was left to live or die. The organ trafficker said he didn't care if the donors lived or died, as long as he got paid. He said they've already come from a nightmare in Syria and Iraq and, in his mind, the organ harvesting is nothing compared to that. That was the atmosphere and the desperation in the air in Beirut, Lebanon, in 2017.

Led by the Spirit

On April 4, 2017, we received an email from World Missions Alliance marked urgent news.

Dear Richard and family,

This is one of the very rare cases in the history of WMA (the second time, to be exact) that we've felt the need to postpone a scheduled trip. Our Argentina trip, May 22 to June 1, is now postponed until February 5-15, 2018. When the conflict of schedule dates occurred in the planning process for the Argentina trip, we knew the reason for this was God's perfect timing for everything WMA does. This truth became clearer as we visited Lebanon with the purpose of encouraging our former pastor of the church in Northern Iraq, Armen.

God opened an incredible and *urgent* door for WMA in Lebanon and we will be taking our first, groundbreaking team on June 19-29.

This team will have very limited openings! If God speaks to your heart about Lebanon, please call us ASAP or respond to this email *here.*

Pastor Armen has lived in Beirut as a refugee for the last year and a half, after some of the tribal leaders in Northern Iraq threatened him for being too effective in evangelism. God has been using him in Beirut in a very powerful way by reaching out to the refugee communities and preaching the Gospel to them.

During our brief time in Beirut, the Lord showed us an extraordinary opportunity for evangelism that was created by the influx of the refugees from Syria and Iraq. They make up almost half of the population of Lebanon today. The main issue that all the refugees in Lebanon face is in spite of the refugee status from the UNHRC (United Nations Refugee Committee), they are considered illegal immigrants in Lebanon. They are not allowed to work or travel and can be thrown in jail by the police at any moment. The refugees rarely venture outside of the settlements where most of them reside.

As we joined pastor Armen in some ministry meetings, we met many former Muslims who just recently gave their hearts to Christ. They witnessed the brutalities of Islam in their home countries and the Gospel message in Lebanon gave them hope. The Christian government in Lebanon makes it safe for them to convert and safe for us to preach the Gospel and distribute Bibles. The local churches invited us to minister in Beirut, Tyre, and Sidon, which are the cities of great scriptural significance and also the cities where desperate people are ready to hear the Gospel message.

We were absolutely astonished by the hunger and the openness in the hearts of the people. The story of a young Syrian teenager, who converted from Islam while still in Syria, and his family spent months looking for a Bible there, was just heartbreaking. Our goal for this first trip will be to help pastor Armen in preaching the Gospel and making sure that each one is equipped with a Bible. We are sending this invitation to a limited group of people, as we need a team of those who are truly called for this mission.

To learn more about this trip, please view the Lebanon 2017 webpage for further details. Please let us know ASAP if you feel the call.

Blessings,
—Chuck & Helen Todd
President & Vice President, World Missions Alliance

As I read the email, I immediately felt the calling to go on this trip. I phoned Chuck and he felt like I would be able to do medical missions on this trip. I contacted Danny Skaggs and he was excited to donate the medication we would need for the medical clinic. I told Blane Shuffield, my friend who is a Texas Special Ranger, about the trip and he wanted to contribute to the cost of the medical clinic itself. I did research on the internet; Lebanon had procedures in place for a doctor from another country to practice medicine in Lebanon. Unfortunately, there was not time to go through the usual procedures if we were going to be ready in time for the mission. I explained my findings to Chuck Todd. He said the churches we would be working with have some influence with the government in Lebanon.

Lebanon was historically a Christian nation. Chuck said their system was overwhelmed with the Syrian refugee crisis. Because of that, he felt that the Lebanese government would be open to help for the refugees. On June 14, 2017, Chuck sent me a letter in Arabic explaining that I would be giving free medical care in a church clinic and brought medications that would be given free of charge to the patients. This letter was on the letterhead of the Nazarene Church in Lebanon.

Christian Heritage

Prior to 1948, when Israel became a nation, Lebanon was a majority Christian nation. When Israel was founded in 1948, a huge influx of Muslim refugees came from Israel to Lebanon. This changed the percentages. It also led to the formation of the terrorist organization called Hezbollah, whose headquarters were in Lebanon. Since its formation, Hezbollah has been attacking Israel from southern Lebanon. This led to the invasion of southern Lebanon by Israel. Also, there was a Lebanese civil war.

Usual Resistance

As with other mission trips, the enemy made attempts to distract me from the trip or discourage me. The devil will use people in an attempt to kill, steal, and destroy. This one was a test of my resolve as it threatened not just me or my medical license, but my family's livelihood.

A few weeks before this trip, the owners of a new medical management company that was bidding to run the clinic I had built up over the last five years reached out to me. I had longstanding relationships with the patients and my work at this clinic provided half of my current income. The new management company offered me an opportunity to work with them and continue as the doctor under their management, with everything staying as it had been. I agreed to this and the new company won the contract for the clinic with the lowest bid. Just a few days before the trip, I learned that in fact the new company intended to use midlevel practitioners (nurse practitioners) instead of me, and they never intended to use me. Due to their deceitful practices, I was about to lose 50 percent of my income.

If I went on the trip, my efforts to find a new position to replace that income would be delayed until after I returned. And I had used my own funds to purchase the plane ticket. And yet I still felt called to go as I worried about supporting my family. I decided to trust in God that it would work out and I would go on the trip.

Despite that, I was excited about what God was going to do in Lebanon. I remember as a 19-year-old in 1983, I heard that some terrorist jihadists used truck bombs on a military base of peacekeepers and killed 241 U.S. Marines. That was really my only reference point for Beirut prior to the email.

My wife, my youngest son, and my oldest daughter dropped me off at the airport where I met another missionary team that was headed to Thailand. One member of the mission team leaving for Thailand was my oldest daughter Morgan's then-boyfriend Ryan (they were married later in 2018). The flight to Houston was uneventful and I had no problems getting on the connecting flight from Houston to Paris.

Setup for Favor

Before we took off, I asked a flight attendant if they might have a free mask, so I could take a nap. She said they did not have any. As we were flying over the Atlantic Ocean, the overhead speakers crackled to life with a message from the flight attendant: "Is there a doctor on the plane?" I told the flight attendant that I was a doctor. She led me to a woman sprawled out on the floor between the seats. Another woman was kneeling by the ill woman's head. An oxygen mask was being applied. I explained that I was an ER doctor.

The anxious woman kneeling said that she was also a doctor. She was visibly relieved to relinquish care. The downed woman was in a stupor. I assessed her airway, breathing, circulation, and neurological status. I elevated her legs to help with circulation to her brain. She responded favorably. She reported she had suffered severe headaches recently. She had not seen a doctor yet for the headaches. She also was near her menstrual period. She had a negative history otherwise. If we had been in the emergency room, I would have sent her for a CAT scan. I instructed the flight attendant to give acetaminophen and Ibuprofen to the patient. Fortunately, we were able to move her to a row of seats where she was able to lie down. She remained stable for the duration of the flight.

When I returned to my seat a gift pack was in my seat. It contained a mask and other goodies. A flight attendant told me she had discreetly left that in my seat to thank me for my help with the patient. Several minutes later, another flight attendant gave me a second gift pack. Later, a flight attendant told me that sometimes doctors are given free air miles for helping on flights. I told her that would be great. I explained that I was on my way to help refugees in Lebanon. Before the end of the trip, another flight attendant came by and asked if I had a copy of my medical license so they could get me my free air miles.

City of Contrast

The sun was rising as we flew into Beirut. The Mediterranean Sea had white objects floating in it. There was so much debris that I became concerned there had been a shipwreck or plane crash. Miles later, it became apparent that this was actually trash from Beirut that had been thrown into the sea. As we came toward the coast, I saw the city built alongside the Mediterranean Sea. We flew low over some natural rock formations in the water. One formation was a natural arch and the other was a pillar next to it. These natural rock formations were beautiful. The plane landed at the Beirut airport right next to the sea. I was struck by the reality that Beirut is a city of contrasts: miles of trash floating in the sea next to these beautiful stone formations.

Hide Me

In the Beirut airport, I retrieved my ungainly suitcase and large duffel bag full of medication. I was a little concerned about whether they would search everything and detain my medication. My last medical mission trip was to Ethiopia, and one of our duffel bags of medicine was held up for four days. I did not want that to happen again. Three ladies on our mission team were on the flight from Frankfurt to Lebanon with me. We all started walking toward a soldier that was overseeing the exit. He had just flagged someone to his left so that all of his luggage could be opened and searched. I was concerned I would be an obvious target for searching.

As we approached, a large crowd suddenly met with us as we approached the soldier and he looked overwhelmed. He flagged all of us through without inspection. I understand, after my experience in Ethiopia, how that was a very significant blessing. On the way to the hotel I noticed old, concrete buildings riddled with machinegun bullet holes standing next to new, high-rise office buildings that had signs saying, "office space for lease." Again, it was a city of contrasts—visible evidence of invisible forces of destruction side by side with forces there to create and bring hope. I was surprised to see so many new luxury vehicles driving in the crazy traffic. Mercedes, BMWs, and Porsches drove alongside barely running clunkers and the multitude of pedestrians.

Rules of Engagement

When we arrived at the hotel, Chuck met with the group in the lobby. On every trip that I had been on with Chuck, he laid down the ground rules for the team—i.e., the rules of engagement. Different countries have different rules of engagement. In Muslim countries, you could be imprisoned indefinitely for sharing the Gospel on the streets. However, what you did in churches was allowed because that was considered "part of your religion." The free medical clinics gave an extra measure of favor and protection with the governments, but diplomacy was still critical to survival and success.

Special rules of engagement sometimes apply. Egypt has Sharia law on the streets and, for the last three years, martial law under a dictator. Chuck also specifically explained how unity was of great importance, and that the devil would like to cause division and strife to incapacitate the mission team. Everyone was expected to go out of their way to foster unity and not hold any offense.

Speaking of "offenses," Chuck repeatedly said, "Do not say any derogatory comments about any other religion. God's Kingdom is righteousness, peace, and joy in the Holy Spirit. Offending groups of people is not the way of God. We are here to speak the truth in love. Our focus should be on the goodness of God. It's the goodness of God that leads men into repentance. Our spiritual enemy uses tools like accusations, strife, misunderstanding, name-calling, deception, and division; those are not the ways of God."

Flexibility

Chuck Todd explained many times during the orientations of new mission teams that flexibility is key. With missions there will always be surprises. During mission trips, we have experienced flat tires, bad weather, roads blocked by landslides, illness, lost luggage, flight delays, etc. The mindset of a missionary should be like that of a U.S. Marine: adapt, improvise, and overcome. This mindset must be meshed with a singleness of purpose, teamwork, and submission to authority. The U.S. Marine also commits to a cause greater than himself. Speaking of surprises, I told Chuck about my patient on the flight to Frankfurt. Chuck said they would probably throw 15,000 airline miles at me for helping, because that had been his experience.

Israel and the Jews

Chuck oriented us to make sure we did not mention any neighboring countries (Israel) or the groups of people that live in the country to the south (Israelis or Jews). Again, I was not aware that Israel and Lebanon were in a ceasefire, but still at war, until I signed up for this mission trip. Chuck also explained that we happened to be in Beirut for the first day of Ramadan.

Jesus Is Confrontational

Ramadan! It sounded like a terrible idea to do a Christian mission trip to a Muslim country during Ramadan. By the way, Lebanon is the headquarters of Hezbollah, a radical Muslim terrorist network. This timing was another example of what it means to trust in the Lord and not lean on our own understanding. In reality, those who were devout Muslims were fasting during daylight, abstaining from food and water. They were indoors, panting and trying to survive all day long. The weather was 100 percent humidity and 96 degrees Fahrenheit every day. Any Islamic terrorists would be flat on their backs and not causing any mischief. During Ramadan, many people are praying and fasting and sincerely seeking spiritual truth. Many were praying to have spiritual dreams. This is fertile soil for God to meet them in dreams and visions, and for their hearts to be open to the Gospel.

Gospel Spread Despite Persecution

I was thrilled to see Pastor Armen, who was a refugee from Kurdistan. His family, and every family of his worship team from the church in Kurdistan, had received death threats from the Yezidi. They had all been living as refugees in Lebanon for over two years.

Good Works

They had not been idle. The refugee children from Syria and Iraq were academically behind the children of Lebanon. The Lebanese school system would not allow children to join the system if they were behind academically. The Beirut Nazarene Church and the worship team, along with Pastor Armen's family, offered free remedial academic classes to the refugee children. Many children were mainstreamed into the Lebanese public school system. This gave the refugee families hope for their children's futures. They were showing the love of Christ to these Muslim strangers. The Muslim mothers started coming to the church services to find out why these strangers would invest time and energy in their children. Many of the Muslim parents had been attending church services for several years but had not yet committed to Christ.

We started the medical clinics in a church. Our first day was a half-day clinic. I was very disappointed that only 19 patients showed up. Pastor Armen explained that it was the fasting from food and water, and the severe heat and humidity, causing people to stay indoors. He assured me that, once the word got out about the free clinics, we would be swamped with patients. And that's what happened. We had refugees from all over Syria and Iraq come to our clinic. We even had one believer from Madagascar. We didn't have to go to Syria and Iraq to help desperate people; the desperate people were coming to us!

I remembered when Karen Dunham, a missionary, had visited our church in West Texas a year before. She called people forward who were scheduled to go on mission trips. As I started to walk to the front of the church with the crowd, Karen turned to look at me and said, "The Lord says, Doctor, 'I told you that I've given you the nations.'" The nations were literally coming to us—we did not have to go to the nations. I was amazed at how easy the harvest was. I would present the Good News, the Best News in the World, after treating each patient. One by one, they would readily pray a prayer of salvation to receive Yeshua (Jesus) as their Lord and Savior.

The medical problems were what we expected. We gave out all the vitamins we brought. We saw many people with rashes and hair loss due to vitamin deficiencies. We gave out all the parasite medication we brought. The Syrian refugees and Iraqi refugees had to eat or drink whatever they could find to survive, and many had parasites. We also saw bladder infections, sinus infections, and bronchitis. One older lady from Nineveh had a severe case of pneumonia in her upper left lung. Out of over 200 patients, I only saw five that had diabetes. There were also a few cases of high blood pressure. While it is extremely satisfying to meet their medical needs, it is much more rewarding to meet their spiritual needs by introducing them to Christ.

Epic Stories

The stories the refugees shared were epic. One mother with four children talked about being threatened by ISIS as they escaped on foot through the deserts of Syria. They had walked through the desert while being periodically harassed by ISIS fighters. The family then had to hike over mountains in their sandals, through the snow, to the other side where we were in Beirut. A 27-year-old Syrian believer, with a tattoo of a cross on his neck and on his arm, explained that his whole family had been murdered in Syria; he was the sole survivor. He was a regular member of the worship team and youth department at the Nazarene church in Beirut.

An elderly couple from Nineveh came to the clinic. When I shared the Good News with them, they said that they were Christians. The husband said, "Of course we are Christians. We would not have survived if we weren't." A mother had five small children, all with severe hearing loss. They had lived through part of the war in Syria and the sounds of explosions had damaged everyone's hearing. The mother had an outdated hearing aid in her right ear, although she had profound hearing loss in both ears. One of her children had the matching hearing aid in the left ear, although the girl had profound hearing loss in both ears. The other children also had profound hearing loss but no

THE DOCTOR'S TRAVEL JOURNAL

hearing aids. We prayed for them and they prayed to receive Christ as Lord. It is the goodness of God that leads man to repentance.

We had a team effort in the medical clinics. Part of the mission team would do triage. Then the patients were invited to a prayer room where they were prayed with and all questions were answered. Finally, they would come to see me for a medical exam and treatment, with an interpreter who was a local believer. At that time, I made sure that I shared the Good News with each person. Most were Muslim when they came in the room. Everyone was a believer when they left the room.

Relief From the Pain

After my trip to Duhok, in November 2014, I was especially aware of the Kurdish people who came to the clinic. An 18-year-old Kurdish man came to the clinic because he heard there was free medical care in the neighborhood. He had no prior connection to the church and had not heard of the clinics until the day he came. He had been having wrist pain for one week. We saw him for his wrist pain and then shared the Good News. He prayed to become a Christian. We prayed and his wrist pain was relieved.

A lady who was treated in the clinic and accepted Jesus returned later, with her husband in a wheelchair. He had stepped on an IED and was paralyzed from a cervical spine injury. I shared the Best News in the World with the man and he said he wanted to receive the gift of life. I led him in a prayer of salvation. The couple wanted our team to pray for him. Five of us encircled him. We anointed him with oil and with our hands on him began to pray. I led in English while others prayed in tongues. When I began to lose steam, I called out another's name and they prayed in English while I joined the others praying in tongues. We kept trading off for 30 minutes. The man kept trying to get up and move his feet. A crowd had gathered to watch. Much faith was exerted. He squeezed my hands with his and was grimacing with the effort to move. When we finished praying, I told him that God can finish what

He starts and not to give up. Instead of disappointment, his eyes were bright with hope and thankfulness. I did not expect to see him again.

Dreams and Visions

Joel 2:28 KJV:

> And it shall come to pass afterward, that I will pour out my spirit upon all flesh; and your sons and daughters shall prophesy, your old men shall dream dreams, your young men shall see visions . . .

That happened on this trip. I met "the three sisters" from Jamaica during a mission trip in Argentina. In Lebanon, the oldest was 91 years old and the twins were 90. Due to storms, they had flights canceled and were stranded in a New York airport for several days. They persevered and arrived three days late in Lebanon. Pastor Armen had a list of Muslim families who requested home visits so they could talk privately about Christ and be prayed for. The three sisters awoke their first morning in Beirut and went to visit a Muslim home.

When the Muslim hostess saw the ladies at her door, she could hardly contain herself. She explained to the translator that a man had appeared in her living room the night before during a dream. The man was wearing "the whitest white robes and the dark room lit up with his presence. The man held up three fingers and said, 'Three women will be coming to your home tomorrow to tell you who I am.'"

When the sisters told the family about Christ, the family became Christians.

Another Muslim mother came to the medical clinic. At each station, she asked the believers to pray for her son. He was in Syria and she had not heard from him in five years. She prayed with me to ask Jesus to come into her heart and be in charge of her life.

Later, three members of our team made a visit to her home. They answered questions about Christ and prayed for her and her son again. The next day, the mother's husband was so encouraged that he said he was going to Syria to find their son. The husband left to drive their little beat-up car across the border into the Syrian war zone, without a lead, to look for his son. Exhausted from fasting, the mother lay down for a nap. She had a dream that a man in the whitest of white robes appeared in her house. The dark room lit up with his presence.

She asked, "Who are you?"

The man replied, "You know who I am. You invited me here. Come to me and go to the church. I am Yeshua. I am Yeshua. I am Yeshua." He then held his hand up and wrote her name on the palm of his hand.

She was awakened by the phone ringing. It was her husband explaining that he had found their son! The son was in a prison but was in good health and good spirits. The father was happy that he was able to spend 15 minutes talking to their son, uninterrupted. The guards had explained that people normally can't visit prisoners but the boy may be released soon. The woman was so excited that she ran barefooted to the church to tell about the miracle. No one was at that church in the morning. We were at a different church doing a medical clinic that day. She came back to the evening service to tell what Jesus had done for her family. She kept repeating "Shukran Yeshua!" ("Thank you, Jesus") in Arabic, with great joy. Walking through the streets of Beirut, many buildings were riddled with machinegun holes. However, I noted that there was no anxiety as we walked through the streets in plain daylight. We felt no imminent threat.

Testimonies Bring Faith

On Saturday, June 24, 2017, I met with Chuck Todd. We were discussing how the trip was going. I explained to him that we were seeing many salvations but few miraculous healings. In Egypt, it seemed like everybody that we prayed for was healed immediately. I explained that I could feel a resistance to healing when I prayed for people. An atmosphere, a culture of faith, was present for salvations, but there was a faith against healings. We were in the Nazarene church, which promoted salvation and living a holy life, but did not focus on the miraculous or healings. As we talked, certain truths bubbled to the surface. We discussed how Matthew 13:57-58 showed why Christ was prevented from doing many miracles.

Egypt had faith for the miraculous because their society and culture believed in the miraculous. They had the mountain that moved in their geology books and in their history for a thousand years. Chuck said it was like the people of Israel had the Red Sea parting that brought them faith in the miraculous. We decided that Beirut needed their Red Sea experience. We discussed that faith comes by hearing and being heard by the Word of God. Chuck decided that, instead of giving a sermon on Sunday, June 25, we would have five people give testimonies of the miracles that God has performed out of his love for people. I said I would like to tell what I saw God do in Iraq for the refugees there. I would also tell about my wife's miraculous pregnancy.

When it was my turn to speak during the Sunday night service, I was allotted five minutes. I explained to the audience that Yeshua (Jesus) loves them. I said Christ died so they could have an abundant life with God. I gave examples of God's love for people. I told about several miracles in Iraq. Here is what I told them about Iraq:

The first night we were in Iraq, back in November 2014, part of our team was visiting a Muslim home to answer questions and pray for the people. While they were at the home, the family received a phone call from a loved one in Syria. The phone call was asking for prayer for a loved one in the hospital in Syria, who was dying of terminal cancer. Their loved one was in the hospital, bleeding to death from terminal colon cancer. The doctors had done everything they could and expected her to die within three hours. The first night, our team prayed for that lady over the phone. Nine days later, the last day of our medical clinics on that trip, the first patient that we saw was that woman, who had been miraculously healed. She left the Syrian hospital, traveled across the war zone of Syria, past ISIS, and past the Iraq war zone to come to our church and tell us that God had healed her.

I told the story of another woman whom I met in Iraq. When ISIS came to Mosul, many of the civilians thought the Iraqi government would chase them out within several days, so they stayed hiding in their homes. A mother and daughter were hiding in their home. The mother went to the store for 30 minutes. She came home and found her daughter on fire, barely alive, left in the front yard after being raped. With the help of some neighbors, she took her daughter to the hospital, but the daughter died. The mother fled Mosul to end up in Duhok, 30 miles away, with only the clothes on her back and an envelope of horrifying pictures of her late daughter's burnt body. Her daughter was all the family she had; she had lost everything. She had been crying daily for five months.

We prayed with her. I was prompted by the Lord to tell the mother to give the upsetting pictures to the pastor, so he could deal with them respectfully. Without hesitation she gave the pictures of her daughter's burnt body to the Pastor. You could immediately feel a change in her and in the room. We prayed that God would give her happy pictures to replace the upsetting ones she gave up obediently. When we finished praying, she laughed and said that she had seen her daughter in the arms of Yeshua (Jesus). Her daughter was smiling. With the help of Christ, this woman was able to forgive the unforgivable. She was able to find peace and joy, despite the worst of tragedies.

I told about a young man who came to us paralyzed on his right side, who walked out of the tent with a limp. His limp disappeared as he walked through the crowd in Nepal. This was because God loves him. It showed the people of Nepal the love of Jesus. I did not tell about my wife's miraculous pregnancy because I ran out of time. Other team members gave testimonies of God's miraculous love. During the altar call, approximately 30 people came forward to pray for Jesus to come into their hearts.

Seeds of Faith for Healing and Miracles

The service ended without an invitation to be ministered to at the front. Our mission team lined up at the door to shake people's hands as they left. I walked to the outside courtyard. Two women approached me and began speaking Arabic. I found a translator to help us. The women were a mother and daughter. The daughter had suffered three miscarriages and they wanted to talk to me because I was a doctor, and because of the stories I told. I told them about my wife's miracle pregnancy after 20 years of being married. I showed them a picture of my 8-year-old son who was the product of the miracle pregnancy.

I explained that every year, and every month, my wife thought she was getting further away from her miracle, her dream coming true and her prayers being answered. Now my wife says that every month, and every day, she is getting closer to her prayers being answered and her dream coming true. I explained that God loves these ladies as much as he loves my wife and me. What God will do for my family and me, he'll do for them. God is no respecter of persons. I shared the Good News with the ladies and the daughter prayed to become a Christian. I then asked team members to join me and we anointed her. We prayed for a miraculous and blessed pregnancy, labor, and delivery. When I opened my eyes from praying, a line had formed of people wanting prayer.

The next gentleman to be prayed for was a man with back pain. He explained that he was in so much pain during the service that he could not find a comfortable position. He had been in excruciating pain for a week but had resisted seeing doctors because he wanted to trust in God for his healing. He said his pain was a 10 on a severity scale of 0 to 10. We anointed him and prayed. I told him that faith with works is alive. The Bible says that faith without works is dead. I told him he needed to start moving and to try to touch his toes. He could barely touch his knees initially. He was wincing and grimacing in excruciating pain. He continued, with our encouragement, to move. Five minutes later he was touching his toes repeatedly and jumping up and down, with a smile on his face, reporting that he had been healed.

Our van driver was a member of the church who was a former Muslim. He and a friend who he had invited to church were watching the healing. They said that was the first time they had ever seen a miraculous healing. His Muslim friend wanted to become a Christian after I told him the Best News in the World. I led him in a prayer of salvation. Next, a Christian mother wanted us to pray for her son, a medical student in Canada. She said he had "evil" teachers. We prayed for her son to have success and favor from God. A mother brought her 8-year-old son to us and said that he had cancer. We anointed him and prayed that God would heal the child, in Jesus' name.

Jezebel's Throne

On Monday, June 26, 2017, we loaded into vans to ride to Sidon and Tyre. In Sidon, we walked the sidewalks, praying for mighty works of God to be done, and for the people to repent in Yeshua's (Jesus') name. Also, we came to Jezebel's throne. It was the last day of Ramadan. Because it was a holiday, the gates were closed and locked. While waiting at the gate, one of our team members heard the Lord say "witches." The sign in front of the park was in Arabic and French. Our translator explained that the title of the property was Moon Temple. Fascinating, considering Jezebel worshipped Baal and Asheroth.

I considered how many human sacrifices must have occurred at the site in ancient times. I also considered the fact that Abraham was called out of Ur, where they worshiped the moon god. Our driver did not give up; he tracked down the gentleman with the key to the gate. Our mission team had exclusive access to the grounds, which were a national park. We walked around, and prayed, and broke curses.

Our translator found recently stacked stones at the bottom and top of the remnants of the fortress. He said that was where witches were still practicing witchcraft. He anointed those spots and broke the curses in Jesus' (Yeshua's) name.

Our team loaded into the vans and traveled the highway overlooking the Mediterranean Sea from Sidon to Tyre. We saw immense orange orchards and mile after mile of banana groves adjacent to the sea, with ocean liners anchored offshore. Flags hung from the highway light posts. The red, white, and green Lebanon flags alternated with the yellow flags with green AK-47s of Hezbollah.

Mohammed on the Beach

We ate lunch at an outdoor restaurant overlooking the Mediterranean Sea in Tyre. Most of us ate fish entrées. After the meal, I walked across the beach toward our van with the translator. We ran into a 23-year-old Syrian refugee whose family was murdered by ISIS. He was in a swimsuit on the way to the beach; his name was Mohammed. I shared the Best News in the World with Mohammed and he readily prayed a prayer of salvation, asking Jesus to be in charge of his life. Our team walked the streets of Tyre, praying that great works of God would be done and that His spirit of repentance would fall on the people of Tyre. On the drive back to Beirut, I considered how Mohammed had lost everything but was still trying to make the most of things by going to swim in the sea for free.

On Tuesday, June 27, we had the last medical clinic in the church. More of the same illnesses, more of the epic stories of braving the trials of war, persecution, and terrorism. Many more chose a new life, and hope, with the decision to make Yeshua (Jesus Christ) their personal Lord and Savior. There was more 100% humidity and temperatures in the high 90s, making our clothes stick to us. Satisfaction—we had exhausted our supplies of medicine. I didn't want any leftovers.

Winding Narrow Streets

On Wednesday, June 28, we did some shopping. I saw again the natural rock arch and pillars in the sea, which I had seen from the plane window as well as on pictures, postcards, and playing cards. Later, we attended an evening church service with the church youth department. The youth worship team led the worship. The youths lined up at the altar and our mission team members filed past them one by one, laying on hands, anointing, and praying blessings over them. Afterward, I went outside to stand in the church courtyard. Pastor Armen came out with a cell phone in hand and said he had just received a text from the wife of the man in the wheelchair. They wanted me to come to their house and pray with him again.

191

It was sunset, and Pastor Armen said we had 30 minutes. The wife showed up to lead us to her husband. I had four of the youth join me. We walked away from the church through the winding streets. We walked quietly past small shops. People would stop talking and stare as we passed. It was getting darker and the six-story apartment buildings lining the narrow streets blocked even more of the remaining daylight. We had entered an area where financially challenged neighbors lived hard, nitty-gritty, everyday lives together. I was now lost, beyond the reach of the church or mission team.

We climbed several stories of winding stairs to enter the family's home. It was sparsely furnished and cramped, but every family member had welcoming smiles and nods. We were led to the husband who was lying on his side, on a thin mat over the tile floor. His urine catheter was leading to the bag lying by his head. I knelt beside him to hug and kiss each cheek, which he mimicked simultaneously. The young men with me did the same. Then, in unison, we anointed him and prayed over him. He and his wife expressed their thankfulness again. The wife explained that he could feel his toes for the first time in years. The doors to the balcony were open. An older couple across the street was on their balcony looking in. They were yelling and smiling, and apparently approved of the prayers. On the way back, I walked with each young person in turn. One on one, I explained Holy Spirit baptism. Each said they wanted the baptism. I prayed for them. I led them into praying in tongues, led by the Spirit. They verbalized prayers as we walked back.

Doctor to Doctor

A husband and his pregnant wife were seated next to me on the flight back from Beirut to Frankfurt. The wife had an obvious dread of flying and was hyperventilating as the plane took off. I soon found that the man was an ENT physician, originally from Damascus. He and his wife had moved to Frankfurt three years ago due to the war. He now practiced in a small town outside of Frankfurt. His wife was expecting their first child. They had decided to visit relatives on both sides of the family in Damascus for the first time in three years. They had taken a taxi from Beirut to Damascus and spent precious time with loved ones. His voice choked up and his face showed his distress for the family still in Damascus.

I told him the Best News in the World. He had not heard it before and was interested. I led him in a prayer. The reports of dreams and visions in Beirut caused me to lead him to pray that Yeshua (Jesus) would show him who He was. Turbulence interrupted the prayer at that point. His wife was panicking. He was quickly speaking, hugging her, and trying to calm her. The shouts of "Allah Akbar" behind us added a level of intensity to the experience. The remainder of the trip was less stressful. I gave him a Visa gift card I had in my wallet to buy a baby gift. He wrote his contact information on my plane ticket stub. Back home, I received an email that United had given me 15,000 airline miles for helping the lady on the plane. Chuck was right again.

Photos Taken in Lebanon

The three sisters in Lebanon.

Meeting Mohammad on the beach.

Bullet-ridden Beirut.

Bullet-ridden Beirut apartments.

Farms along the Mediterranean.

Flags of Hezbollah and Lebanon.

Closer view of the stylized assault rifle on the flag of Hezbollah.

Sign for the ruins of Jezebel's temple in Sidon, Lebanon.

197

Ruins of Jezebel's temple in Sidon, Lebanon.

Jezebel's throne in Sidon, Lebanon.

Helen sits on Jezebel's throne.

Lebanon.

Lebanon street sights.

Lebanon street sights.

Street vendor in Sidon.

Praying for patients in Lebanon.

Sign for the Orphan Welfare Society in Sidon, Lebanon.

Street sights in Tyre, Lebanon, 2017.

Street sights in Tyre, Lebanon, 2017.

Street sights in Tyre, Lebanon, 2017.

Street sights in Tyre, Lebanon, 2017.

CHAPTER 7

Lost Boys of Thailand

Then it started to pour! A monsoon, whiting out the surrounding Thai jungle. Still, the people lined up, waiting to be seen. As they waited, one of the nurses came by to ask them what problems they had. She would write the answers down on a card and then give it to me when I saw them. The wind started blowing and the rainwater started misting in underneath the roof on one side. We gathered ourselves and I moved the medicines to try and keep them from getting wet. Meanwhile, every time the wind would switch directions, the community hall full of people would scramble to grab their plastic chairs and move to the other side of the hall, attempting to stay dry. People were excitedly squealing, laughing, and scrambling back and forth to dodge the wind and rain; it was like we were all on a ride at a waterpark.

We had treated about 20 people when several ladies started talking loudly and excitedly, trying to get our attention. A lady was sitting upright, unresponsive in her chair. Through the translators, we were told that it was a demonic manifestation. She had suffered similar episodes for many years. She had worshipped Akha spirits and performed who-knows-what-all rituals in the past. So we started praying.

Helen was with me; she had spent years as a missionary at an orphanage in Africa, so she'd been around some serious spiritual things. She knows a thing or two about demonic possession, and she laid hands on the sick woman. The noise of rain on the tin roof caused us to pray louder. I anointed her head with oil and we all prayed simultaneously in tongues, English, and Thai. As we prayed, the locals were telling our translator that whenever the woman would have a manifestation, nothing could be done to help. Helen Meyers thought it might be a deaf-mute spirit, as described in the Bible. The lady's eyes were still closed, so I tried to hold them open to check for reactivity, but they just rolled back in her head. She was completely out, but she was not falling out of the chair, so it was not like what I saw in Iraq, where victims of possession were in a rigid catatonic state.

We kept praying while the rain was coming down in sheets. We couldn't see anything outside the building. I had the thought, *Sing a worship song.* I looked at the three ladies with me and asked for a worship song. Emily Dixon started to sing the only song she could think of "Jesus, Jesus, Jesus." Our eyes got big and smiles crossed our faces as we got to the part of the song, "Jesus, Jesus, Jesus, it's like the fragrance after the rain!" We all knew the song, and we knew that it was hand-picked by the Holy Spirit to sing *that* song while the rain whited out the visibility surrounding the building and hammered the tin roof above. We sang that song three times, and then the unconscious woman's eyes opened. Her eyes darted nervously from person to person as she muttered in bursts of phrases to no one in particular.

How did I get here? Let me start at the beginning . . .

Hill Tribe People

I received an email from the WMA about an upcoming trip to Thailand. For the first time, I was made aware of the indigenous people of Thailand called the hill tribe people. They are not allowed to have a national ID card by the Thai government and are not accepted as Thai citizens.

They cannot access the national healthcare system as a result. If one of their children gets appendicitis, the child dies. The hill tribe people live on less than $1 U.S. per day. The average Thai citizen lives on $15 per day. The hill tribe people are at the bottom of the Thai socioeconomic food chain. They are underappreciated and undervalued. They are trapped with no means to escape their current station in life. Thailand is a prostitution and human trafficking hub for Asia, and one in three of the victims are hill tribe people. I felt compelled to bring a medical mission to help these downtrodden people. Even an aspirin or Band-Aid would be more than they currently had. I bought my airline ticket and made the arrangements.

Luke 14:15-24 NIV:

> When one of those at the table with him heard this, he said to Jesus, "Blessed is the one who will eat at the feast in the kingdom of God."

> Jesus replied: "A certain man was preparing a great banquet and invited many guests. At the time of the banquet he sent his servant to tell those who had been invited, 'Come, for everything is now ready.'

> "But they all alike began to make excuses. The first said, 'I have just bought a field, and I must go and see it. Please excuse me.'

> "Another said, 'I have just bought five yoke of oxen, and I'm on my way to try them out. Please excuse me.'

> "Still another said, 'I just got married, so I can't come.'

> "The servant came back and reported this to his master. Then the owner of the house became angry and ordered his servant, 'Go out quickly into the streets and alleys of the town and bring in the poor, the crippled, the blind and the lame.'

> "'Sir,' the servant said, 'what you ordered has been done, but there is still room.'

> "Then the master told his servant, 'Go out to the roads and country lanes and compel them to come in, so that my house will be full. I tell you, not one of those who were invited will get a taste of my banquet.'"

Confirmation

A month before my trip, a new doctor from Lubbock, named Dr. Tran, came to replace me at an Odessa ER for the next shift. He kept staring at me and I started to feel uncomfortable. I was the ER Medical Director at the time. I decided to stick around for a moment and get to know him. I found out he had a wife and two kids, and was a family doctor. For a couple of years, he commuted from Lubbock to work in a Dallas ER. He and his family became burned out due to his absence from the family. He had enjoyed several months' pause from ER work to focus on his family and his passion of stock trading. Recently, the ER company had asked if he could work in Odessa. He told them he would work several days a month in Odessa. He didn't know for how long, since it was a two-hour commute each way.

Eventually the conversation came around to Dr. Tran saying that I look like a missionary doctor he had met in Thailand when he was five years old. He was a refugee in Thailand and said he just couldn't get over how I have the same nose and look exactly like that doc from decades ago. I told him that was amazing because I was going to Thailand on a mission trip in several weeks. Dr. Tran asked if I was a Mormon and I told him no. I told him he has the skill set for medical missions, since most of what we see is family practice/urgent care. Most healthcare is not specialty care. I said he was more equipped than a heart surgeon to do medical missions. Dr. Tran said that his wife, who is a family physician, had told him two months before that she felt like she needed to find her calling, and that she was considering medical missions.

I told Dr. Tran about the miracles and unusual circumstances I have seen. I told him about the 28-year-old man in the Himalayan Mountains, in an area where Buddha was reported to be born and buried, who was paralyzed from a stroke. The man came in paralyzed but walked out of the tent with me while we were praying. Dr. Tran told me I have a calling on my life. I told him we all have a calling, and that he has a calling too. I told him it would be amazing for him to go full circle and to help these people. Tran is a Vietnamese last name, yet he lived in Thailand. He said his family were some of the boat people who escaped Vietnam to Thailand, and became refugees in Thailand.

Although there is still tremendous need and terrible tragedy in Thailand, his life was changed forever as a result of strangers helping him. His children's destinies were changed forever. I told him he could be that guy who is helping change other people's lives forever. Even though one person can't do everything, they can do something. His life would come full circle if he helped refugees. Dr. Tran said this was amazing, and if someone had told him six months ago that he was going to be in Odessa, Texas, doing ER work, he never would have believed it. I told him I'd just written a book about my mission trips. He asked for the title of the book and said he would order it.

I had another overlap with Dr. Tran on May 18, 2018. Dr. Tran and I were changing shifts with each other, since we were both emergency room doctors. I sat down with him for a moment before my shift started. He explained to me that he had finished my book, *Journey of a Medicine Man*, and he had really enjoyed the ending. He told the ER nurse that she needed to order the book for herself because I have documented scenes of demon possession and deliverance that he found fascinating. He also told me that, because of my book, he had tried to look at the World Missions Alliance website with his cell phone.

We went to the computer together and pulled up the World Missions Alliance website. We watched several videos concerning different countries' needs and upcoming mission trips. We watched a two-minute video about an upcoming mission trip to Thailand. Despite annoying buffering, Dr. Tran insisted on waiting for the video to load. After the video, he told me he was having a déjà vu moment. He felt like he'd experienced this before: watching that video of those familiar scenes in Thailand, with me sitting in the chair beside him. While we were watching the videos, I asked him if any of the images looked familiar to him. He said that some of the islands off the coast of Thailand reminded him of an experience when he was five years old.

He and his family were on a fishing boat overloaded with refugees, fleeing from Vietnam to Thailand. There were 168 people on the small fishing boat. When they were out at sea, the boat started to capsize. There are many deserted islands off the coast of Thailand. The captain pulled up to one of those islands and told everybody to get off the boat. Once all of the refugees were on land, the captain took the boat back out to sea. He did not return. The refugees, including infants and elderly, were abandoned on a deserted island without any supplies, even food or water, and without any hope of being able to live there. He said they were all instructed to drink their own urine.

After several days on the island, one of the refugee men decided to swim to another island they could see in the distance. A fishing boat rescued him when he had made it halfway. The fishermen told him the waters were shark infested and he would never have made it to the island.

These fishermen started the process of rescuing the refugees from that island. Dr. Tran told me he could still remember the missionaries giving them canned sardines to eat. The Thailand refugee camp where they stayed looked like many of the images on the World Missions Alliance website: rows of tents and little else. We watched several videos of other trips and then he said he wanted to give back to the people of Thailand. He told me the people of Thailand helped his family in their time of need as refugees. He emptied his wallet of $350 and handed it to me. He asked me to help refugees on my upcoming mission trip in Thailand. Before we parted ways he said, "You never know, 10 years from now I may be going on a mission trip with you."

Confirming Sign

Before I was supposed to fly to Thailand, some unusual events occurred. A rattlesnake got caught under the back door of the emergency room while I was the ER doctor on duty. The X-ray tech and the nurse went out the back door to smoke. When they returned, a rattlesnake was trying to come in with them and it got caught under the closing door. I instantly knew the Lord wanted me to do a prophetic act of a snake's head under my heel. I stomped on the rattlesnake's head with my dress shoe, killing it.

I would not have told anybody else to do that. Normally I would not have done that. I usually use a rock or a shovel. I've killed a lot of snakes. I've never considered stepping on a live rattlesnake. I knew it was a sign from God, but I didn't know what it meant.

Meaning of the Viper

Two weeks later, at the emergency room, I had a one-year-old with an infection in his throat. A structure in the throat called the epiglottis swells, usually due to infection, and can cut off the airway and cause death. He needed to be transferred to the larger hospital, with a stand-by surgical team and specialists on call, across the city. EMTLA laws are written to protect patients. Larger hospitals are required to accept transfers when patients need more resources, i.e., ORs, ICUs, etc. I had phone conversations with three doctors at the county hospital via the recorded transfer service. All agreed to receive the patient in transfer and take the patient to the OR if needed. The appropriate forms were completed, and the patient was sent via ambulance to the larger hospital.

While the patient was en route, I got a call from the pediatrician, Dr. Baraa Alrazzak. He said he changed his mind and was now refusing to accept the patient transfer. He wanted me to send the infant to a city three hours away and bypass the large county hospital where he would be responsible for care. I said the patient is already on the road. I told him the ER doctor, Dr. Webb, accepted the patient. The ENT, Dr. Ralph Cepero, said he would take the patient to the OR if needed. Dr. Alrazzak now wanted the patient to be diverted to another hospital three hours away. I said the infant could die on a three-hour road-trip, due to progression of the epiglottitis.

Dr. Alrazzak was a Muslim living in Houston, working in Odessa to make some extra cash. He felt insecure about his ability to care for the infant. The Friday before I left for Thailand, I received a letter from the Medical Board about a complaint. I found out from the ENT that Dr.

Alrazzak had filed a bogus complaint because I didn't comply with his wishes. The ENT tried to talk the Muslim pediatrician out of filing the complaint a day before I knew about it. The ENT said he told Dr. Alrazzak the transfer saved the infant's life. Dr. Alrazzak told the ENT, too late, he already filed the complaint online the night the patient was transferred.

Crushing the Snake Beneath My Feet

My attorney spoke with both doctors. The ENT wrote a letter to the medical board. He wrote, "I applaud Dr. Bartlett for his astute examination and diagnosis and his quick action," and "This patient had a good outcome due in large part to Dr. Bartlett's thoughtful care."

Dr. Alrazzak, the pediatrician who turned in the complaint, called the medical board and tried to cancel the complaint. He was unable to stop the process. He told my lawyer he would write a letter on my behalf. The letter explained that he felt he had done the wrong thing by turning in the bogus complaint. His letter explained the complaint was not valid, and the care was done correctly in the best interest of the patient. The person who Satan used to make an accusation against me had made peace with me and became my defender.

Moment of Truth

I had a decision to make. Though the doctors had sent letters, the complaint was not dismissed. Once a complaint is filed with the board, it cannot be dismissed and must be investigated fully. The fact that the complaining pediatrician had recanted did not guarantee a positive outcome; the medical board decisions were not always straightforward and good doctors sometimes lost their licenses, in my experience. I did not feel confident that their decision would go my way without action.

The letter from the board said I had 14 days to legally deal with the complaint. The deadline would occur during my trip. I could trust God that He would defend me and go on the mission trip, or I could stay and try to defend myself from the false accusation. Practically, I would not be able to prove my innocence from the other side of the planet.

Because the pediatrician had recanted, even though it was not a formal, legal dismissal of the complaint, I decided to provide what evidence I could in a letter to the board before I left on the trip, and leave the rest in God's hands.

Out of Body Experience

The same night that I had the initial trouble with the Muslim pediatrician, Helen and Chuck Todd, the leaders of the World Missions Alliance, were in New York visiting a church. In the hotel, Helen was walking into the bathroom. Something picked her up from behind. She was being tossed around like a ragdoll and spun around over its head; she didn't know what to do. She felt helpless. She eventually woke up and was back in the bed. She was a little embarrassed to tell anybody about the nightmare, but it was so real to her. She knew it was an out-of-body experience and that evil was targeting her for her good works.

Helen had never had an out-of-body experience before. I believe that she was in the spirit world for a moment. The spirit dimension is sometimes called the second heaven. Spirits do come and go out of our dimension. I've heard other stories of people waking up in the middle of night with something trying to strangle them. They are usually people who are spiritual leaders, maybe not in title, but in action. I believe that these supernatural attacks are an attempt to interrupt impending glorious breakthroughs.

Securing Translators

Helen told me that the first translator she had lined up for the trip had gotten sick and was unavailable. A second translator who lined up fell through as well. Finally, she found a third translator, a woman named Poi, who had experience with World Vision and with translating for medical clinics. Helen felt it was the plan of God that we have that particular translator for the trip.

First Impressions

It was May 25, 2018, and I was on my way to Thailand at last. My last flight went from Japan to Bangkok, where I met the other 19 members of the mission team. Our group was about as diverse as you can get: different races, classes, political affiliations, and nations of origin. The only thing we had in common was that we were all Christians. The team had peace and unity in Christ.

When we got to Bangkok, we stayed in a big hotel. Bangkok was clearly a place where people came to have fun, an international vacation destination. The atmosphere in Thailand was anything goes, chase whatever your pleasure is without a sense of consequence. It was a culture of extreme freedom of choice, without restraint. It was very different from the atmosphere when I was in Egypt or China, where the energy of the place was extremely oppressive. In those countries, you felt the oppressive atmosphere even in the hotel room by yourself. In Thailand, you didn't have that; it was an atmosphere of whatever goes. Though there was a lot of immorality and crime, I did not feel the imminent threat that I felt in Egypt. It also felt like Thailand was wide open to the Gospel; wide open for God to show up, wide open for its people to be saved. It is a fertile ground for ministry.

Jesus Is on the Offensive

Everywhere we saw idols. Thailand has over 60,000 Buddhist temples. Practically every residence had altars to false gods at the entrance. Almost every place of business had altars on display, some fancier than others. They were asking for the blessings of false gods. We passed stores with large varieties of idols and altars to choose from. I noticed a pattern on my journeys: WMA had a knack for visiting places during religious celebrations honoring false gods. Back in June 2017, I was in Lebanon during Ramadan, the important Muslim holiday. Lebanon is the headquarters of Hezbollah, the radical Muslim terrorist group. Also, big events seemed to correlate with the timing of the trips. This would be no exception.

Buddha Day

Now we were in Thailand, which is overrun with Buddhists, during their biggest annual holiday: Besek or Buddha Day. Of course, Besek Day 2018 fell on May 29, right in the middle of our trip. Besek Day celebrates the birth and death of the first Buddha. The holiday is also called Purnima, and it is celebrated on the first full moon of May. While a country full of Buddhists were celebrating idolatry, there we were, a group of Christians leading hundreds of their people to Christ. Starting early in the morning on the 28th, the devotees of Buddhism would get up to bring flowers, candles, and incense to place at the feet of a Buddha idol. The symbolic offering reminds them of the shortness of life and nearness of death. In contrast, we bring the Good News of the Gospel of Jesus Christ, which brings life, not death.

Ambassador

The Bangkok hotel had two storefronts that you walked past on your way in and out of the hotel. The glass showcases were displaying some lovely scarves that I wanted to buy for my wife. I went into the store and the fellow who helped me turned out to be a tailor. He was watching the shop for his cousin who owned the store. Mr. Singh told me about his tailor shop. He makes hand-sewn suits and sport coats. Considering the local climate of 100-degree temperatures and 100 percent humidity, a sport coat was the last thing on my shopping list. However, a sport coat did catch my eye. Mr. Singh told me he had made the jacket for the Austrian Ambassador, who was out of town for two weeks. He insisted I try it on. It fit perfectly. He asked if it would be wrong for him to sell it to me, since it fit me so well. He said he could make another jacket for the ambassador before he returned. I agreed to buy the coat, since it fit me perfectly and he was selling it to me for a good price. Then, I told him the Best News in the World and he accepted the Lord right there. Poi, our translator, agreed to drop a Bible by for him that evening.

Hope Church

On May 27, 2018, we attended Hope Church of Bangkok, which was becoming a mega church and a powerful spiritual force in Thailand. They had 77 satellite churches they had started in the 77 provinces of Thailand, which is astonishingly prolific. As soon as we arrived in Bangkok, we went to a church service at their main church. It is a non-denominational church and they were rapidly growing.

During the Sunday morning service, our mission team was allowed to address the congregation. I spoke about some of the things we'd seen in Iraq, Egypt, Nepal, and other countries. I encouraged the people there to continue to follow Christ and his mandate of the Great Commission. They had a healthy children's ministry at their churches. They would write their own dramas for the children and adults to act out. They were not ashamed of the Gospel of Jesus Christ. They clearly held up the standard that Jesus is the answer, and that Jesus is the way to have peace and hope.

The message was also obviously resonating with the people in Bangkok. People of all sectors of society were involved in the church. There were the very poor and the very rich, all praying together in the congregation. We met some doctors among the churchgoers who were involved in providing free medical clinics to the poor and in rural areas. The church had a vision for international missions. Hope Church has church plants in Los Angeles, California, and in Houston, Texas. Imagine that! Thailand sending Christian missionaries to America! They also have a church plant in Cameroon, Africa.

Jesus Loves the Children

May 28, 2018, we drove through the impoverished streets of Pattaya, an international tourist city. We filed out of the vans in front of a modest Christian daycare. Across the street were high walls enclosing a Buddhist monastery compound, which covered several city blocks. The neighborhood was the poorest of Pattaya. Most adults were addicts and many were used for the sex trade, which caters to the international tourists. The kids were dropped off for the free childcare provided by the nonprofit Christian organization. It provided hours of safe sanctuary for their kids in a very dangerous world. The children all wore free, lavender-colored polo shirts from the daycare, and would receive several free meals each day. They would play games and learn Bible stories about Jesus from the Danish missionaries. The Danish missionary said three children had accepted Christ the week before we visited. Remarkable, considering the environment in which these kids were immersed. His wife and daughter had also been working alongside the local Thai pastor and his wife, who led worship on Sundays with the same sparse facility. Our team taught "Jesus Loves Me" and other songs, with accompanying hand gestures. Fun with balloons and games followed. A short Bible teaching was given by several team members. An offering was accepted for the ministry from our mission team. I delivered Dr. Tran's gift of money to the local pastor to help the children.

Reports of Revival

The Danish missionary shared some exciting news. Reports of a revival starting in north Thailand were making it to Pattaya and Bangkok in the South. I was excited because we were about to travel to the neglected people of the north. The missionary pointed out that the Gospel had been preached 200 years ago in north Thailand, and then in the east. The revival seemed to be following the same pattern as the seeds of the Gospel that were planted there 200 years before.

Communion

We had different team members lead the communion each day. One morning, a team member named Sheila Ruffin was leading the communion and passing out the sacraments. She made the point that the Ark of the Covenant is symbolic of us because we carry the presence of the Lord.

Frauds and Fakes

She read Proverbs 9:1-6, and read out of John, about the bread of life. She told us about a carving she saw on a building: the false god Dagon, who was worshiped in the Philistine land, with the head of a human and the tail of a fish. In the carving, Dagon was looking at the moon. Sheila pointed out that in the Old Testament Bible story, the Philistines captured the ark and they put it before the idol of Dagon. In the morning, all that was left of Dagon was his fishtail on the ground in front of the Ark of the Covenant.

I noticed a lot of gold paint on the signposts and statues along the streets. Pictures of the Thai king in gold-painted frames were at major intersections in every city. The average income for a citizen in Thailand is $15 per day. The gold paint was an attempt to create the illusion of prosperity. The pictures of the Thai king at every major intersection in every city was an attempt to create the illusion that he was present and taking care of his people. In reality, people came from around the world to use and abuse the Thai people. The impoverished Thai people were being victimized via the drug trade, human trafficking, and in manipulation for offerings to Buddhist monks.

Chinese Given Bibles Outside of China

We went to Pattaya, a town on the coast, and we met someone there with a ministry of passing out Chinese Bibles to the Chinese tourists. China had developed a wealthy middle class, prone to going on vacations in other countries. One of the big destinations is Thailand, because you get so much for your money. One pier in Pattaya, which has some restaurants and boat rides, has 5,000 Chinese tourists on it every day. So we took stacks of Bibles and held big signs they handed to us that said "Jesus Loves You" in Mandarin, English, and Russian. We were handing out the Bibles to anyone who was willing to accept them. Almost everybody we saw there was Chinese. We ended up passing out 455 Bibles in just a couple of hours. Several of the Chinese folks walking by looked at me, said thank you, and gave me a thumbs up. It was clear that they were Christians, even though they were from mainland China. Others would mock us, or they'd read the signs and start laughing. The most zealous person passing out Bibles was an 18-year-old man named John, from mainland China. He was literally sprinting to get more Bibles and then running back onto the pier. He was in heaven, passing out Bibles to these Chinese people. He definitely left us all in the dust as far as passing out Bibles. I was totally frustrated with my own efforts; I think I had two people grab a Bible out of my hands in all that time. John said it was a highlight of his trip.

Kindness

After we passed out the Bibles on the pier, we did a prayer walk through the red-light district. It consisted of a neighborhood with a main street designed for pedestrians, near the pier. I was shocked to see tourists, including mothers with their little kids in hand, walking down those streets. Helen bought a bunch of roses from a street vendor so the ladies on our team could hand a rose to the ladies working in front of the brothels. I told them I thought it would be a bad idea for a man to be handing them anything. We let the ladies give those poor women roses and hugs as we were walking down the street, praying.

Visions

Paula Bobb, one of the mission team members, lives in Toronto, Canada. She grew up in the Caribbean and was exposed to the occult practices of voodoo there. She had frequent visions. On our way to Chiang Rai, she had three visions that she told me about. She saw tadpoles, which symbolized unclean spirits. She saw a cigarette with smoke coming from the end of it, which symbolized the wrong prayers that were going up from Thailand into the spirit world. Then she saw a huge demon on a pier. I recalled, while we were passing out Bibles on the pier of Pattaya, a Chinese man brought out an amplified speaker setup with a guitar and microphone. He started singing traditional communist songs and you could feel a shift in the atmosphere. He was being extremely loud and distracting. That's when she said she saw the huge demon on the pier. I immediately started praying in the Spirit when the communist music began, and I am sure that other team members did as well. After a few minutes, the music stopped.

Helping Carry the Weight

The small, in-country flight from Bangkok to Chiang Rai had serious weight restrictions on luggage, and with all of the medicine in them, my bags were seriously overweight. Two at a time, mission members came to my hotel room with their carry-on luggage in hand. They would knock at my door, come and open their bags, and I would dole out some meds to disperse the weight. After 10 separate pairs coming and going from my room to take some of the medicine, I mused what someone watching security cameras thought.

Shanda Rivera and her daughter, D'je, live in Chicago. D'je took the most medicine. I was impressed how willing they were to help carry the medicine. They had packed their luggage the lightest of all 20 people on the team on purpose, in anticipation of helping with this situation. Shanda had gone on medical missions before and had taken medicine and things of that nature in the past, so she said it wasn't that unusual. She said she recognized they were in a foreign country so all things like that could have a risk, but she trusted in her brothers and sisters in Christ, the other people on the missions team. She had to hope and have faith that she wouldn't get thrown in a Thai prison for some strangers. I agreed it was an unknown risk; I had no idea what to expect. However, I appreciated her willingness to go with the flow and I knew it was totally by faith. D'je's blue carry-on was full of only medicine. Shanda and D'je agreed they would stick close to me, so I could offer explanations if airport security asked any questions. I laughed and agreed that would be best.

Busted

All 20 mission members with their bags waited patiently in the airport security line. One by one, each placed their bags on the conveyer for X-ray. Each picked up their carry-on luggage and walked toward the gate. The Bangkok TSA asked D'je if the blue carry-on sitting on a counter was hers. She looked at her mom and nodded yes. I was thinking it couldn't really be happening; there were 20 people, what were the odds that they would have picked the one bag that was totally full of medicine? Other team members had a little bag of antibiotic or ibuprofen, but D'je's bag was totally packed with medicine. I walked over to stand by D'je while the TSA agent was having difficulty unzipping the bag. Shanda walked up to her other side and helped the agent unzip the bag. I was amused to notice that, since I was white, Shanda was black, and D'je was clearly mixed race, we must have looked like a little family standing there together.

When the bag opened, I thought, *Oh my goodness, all I see is medicine!* We were totally shocked when the agent reached in the bag underneath the medicine and pulled out a bottle of bug spray. The agent was clearly trying to scold us in Thai because the bottle was too big. We nodded our heads in unison and motioned for the agent to throw the bug spray in the trashcan. The agent turned to throw the bug spray in the trash. With one smooth motion, Shanda closed the lid of the suitcase and zipped it shut. Without speaking or looking at each other, we picked up our carry-on bags and walked away from the agent and into the terminal. After a few minutes, we had the courage to make eye contact with each other. We didn't speak about the event until we were seated at the gate, waiting to board our plane. Shanda was surprised that the bug spray was an issue, because it had passed TSA inspections in three major airports on the way there. Shanda and I were surprised that the agent didn't even acknowledge the medicine.

Thirty-five years ago, when I was a teenager, I read a book called *God's Smuggler* by Brother Andrew with John and Elizabeth Sherrill (Chosen Books, Expanded Edition, 2015). He smuggled Bibles into the

USSR. The guards would look through all of his luggage, and they would totally overlook the Bibles they were supposed to confiscate, as though they didn't even see them. I felt like we had that same experience on the Thailand trip. It seemed to be a showing of God's sense of humor, like He had picked one of the most obvious possible problems to show that He had it covered.

Elephants

We were in Thailand on tourist visas, so we had to make sure we looked like tourists. Naturally, we decided to take one of the hill tribes up on their elephant rides. We got up on a big platform to climb onto the bench on the elephant's back. Two people sat side by side on the back of the elephant. An elephant driver sat on the elephant's neck, right behind the elephant's head. The driver would kick the back of its ears to direct the elephant left or right. We got to ride the elephant on a hillside. The steep dirt path was just wide enough for the elephant's feet. Several times our elephant thought the vines and leaves hanging out over the cliffside were irresistible. That was when I got uncomfortable, since it didn't seem like the elephant driver was in control and the elephant was reaching out, getting closer and closer to the edge with his big feet. I could clearly imagine tumbling down the mountainside with an elephant on top of me.

It was beautiful hill country scenery. Then the ride went down the other side of the mountain and through the river. It was about $6 for the ride, which was well worth it. I would have paid a lot more for a longer ride, but God didn't bring me there to ride elephants.

I did have several revelations about elephants, though. One was it's not natural for elephants to walk on steep hillsides. I think they're made for the flat river valleys. I felt like that elephant was totally oblivious to the possibility of rolling down that mountainside. Without a lot of kicking and screaming by the elephant driver, the elephant might have tumbled. I don't think he would have been up there on that hill in the first place if he wasn't forced to be up there. That explains why on Nat Geo we don't see elephants on tops of mountains.

Street Ministry

Luke 15:4-10 NIV:

> "Suppose one of you has a hundred sheep and loses one of them. Doesn't he leave the ninety-nine in the open country and go after the lost sheep until he finds it? And when he finds it, he joyfully puts it on his shoulders and goes home. Then he calls his friends and neighbors together and says, 'Rejoice with me; I have found my lost sheep.' I tell you that in the same way there will be more rejoicing in heaven over one sinner who repents than over ninety-nine righteous persons who do not need to repent.

> "Or suppose a woman has ten silver coins and loses one. Doesn't she light a lamp, sweep the house and search carefully until she finds it? And when she finds it, she calls her friends and neighbors together and says, 'Rejoice with me; I have found my lost coin.' In the same way, I tell you, there is rejoicing in the presence of the angels of God over one sinner who repents."

We went to a primitive Akha village in Thailand. Many homes had thatched roofs and the streets were dirt paths. The community building where we met was about 200 feet long and 40 feet wide. It was a concrete slab surrounded by five-foot concrete block walls. Above the wall was three feet of open air beneath the tin roof. We got out of the vans and unloaded some Thai Bibles and Thai Bible tracts to hand out. Decades before, missionaries passing out Bible tracts from the United States in the USSR resulted in Helen Todd, our team leader, accepting the Lord. So, we were going to pass out Bible tracts—cold-turkey street ministry in a hill tribe village, where we didn't speak the language. The local Akha translator told us the village had a small church and that everybody in that village was Christian. We discovered that was not true.

223

While we were at the community center, we saw a very old woman walk in from the village with two young women. The three women walked in while we were still talking, just because they were curious. Later, after we were told to grab some Bibles and hit the streets, I saw the same lady standing close to me. I asked Poi, the translator, to help me. I told the elderly lady the Best News in the World. She hadn't heard the news before and she wanted to accept Jesus, so we led her in a prayer of salvation. I admit that I don't generally like street ministry. I had come to Thailand to offer medical clinics and share the Good News in the clinics. We carried more Bibles and Bible tracts with us into the streets.

With the help of our translators, we led a few people on the streets to the Lord. On the way back, we walked past a home with a thatched roof, its walls made of bamboo slats. Space between the slats allowed airflow. It stays around 100 percent humidity there and is always hot, so the hope is to catch even a slight breeze so you don't suffocate.

I wanted to get a picture of the house. I asked Poi to take a picture of me in front of the house. As I was handing my camera to her, a lady walked out of the house and we waved at her. She beckoned for us to come into her house. I had to duck to get through the three-foot-tall doorway. The house was framed in bamboo and the floors were made of packed mud. I had to stand in the middle of the space in order to stand upright because of the low ceiling/roof. Surprisingly, there was a TV on in the corner of the living room with a soccer game at a tie. I wished terribly that I could be getting a video of the unbelievable scene. I knew I shouldn't use my cell phone to take a picture inside her home because that could be offensive. Instead I shared with her, and her brother who came in a bit later, the Best News in the World. They prayed to become Christians. We eventually headed back to the community center. Across the dirt road from the community center, there was a man sitting in the courtyard of his concrete block home. He was slicing bamboo to make broom material. He saw us looking at him and waved us into the courtyard. The translator told us the man was already a believer, but he wanted us to pray for his faith to be stronger.

He told us he still made mistakes, and he wanted to very humbly ask for us strangers to pray for him. You don't see that extreme humility in the United States very much. I prayed for him.

Finally: Medical Care

As I was getting into the van, one of the local translators excitedly ran up to me and said there was a patient waiting for me—a lady with asthma who needed help. They had told her about me, so she was on her way to the clinic in the community center to get my help. Before I knew it, I was treating six people. The lady was so excited that she could get medical care without an ID card she had started to spread the news. Finally, I was doing what I came to do! After treating six patients, the spontaneous medical clinic was interrupted.

Interrupted

Helen Todd told the team to load up to go to another town, 20 minutes down the road. We were scheduled to visit an orphanage in a larger town that was 20 miles away. I was frustrated that people were starting to show up, seeking the very care that I came to provide, and I had to load my medicine up and leave them in the lurch. We drove to the other town and heard that the orphans had a singing presentation to perform for us.

Back for Clinic

I asked Helen if I could go back to the small Akha village. I told her the people there were lining up for medical care and that was why I came. I was frustrated and she knew it.

She simply said, "Okay."

Three women returned with me to the Akha village, to provide a medical clinic. Emily Dixon was the 22-year-old nurse from Arkansas. Helen Meyer used to go to church with my family in Odessa, before she moved to Oklahoma. Poi was our Thai translator. We headed back to that little village. When we pulled up to the community center I got my

225

medicine bag and we all walked around the corner. But now there was a padlock on the door to the community center and nobody was around anymore. We didn't know how we were going to do this.

Announcing the Free Clinic

I looked around. Across the little dirt road, I saw the fellow we had prayed for earlier, standing in his courtyard. I asked Poi to tell him I am a doctor, here to offer free medical care to anyone in need. The man's wife ran out of their courtyard with keys to unlock the building. He brought stacks of lightweight plastic chairs to the building. Next, he climbed up on the roof of his house and started hooking wires together. Nurse Emily got out her cell phone and started recording what was happening. It was just like you see in movies about World War II or the Vietnam War. The man had a speaker hidden in the trees behind his house and it started cutting in and out, crackling to announce the free medical clinic. The Akha words were bouncing off the surrounding hills and resounding through the valley. Everyone in the village was hearing his message; sound really carried in those hills. In no time, we had over 50 people hurry into the building. They were so excited to get medical care at last, it was a dream come true for many of them. Excited chatter filled the building as we were trying to keep it orderly. We were surprised to meet a handsome, early 20s, tall, Caucasian fellow named Joshua from Colorado, living in the Akha village with his pregnant Akha wife. Joshua and his wife and mother-in-law offered to translate Thai to Akha.

Invitation

I waved my arms and got everyone's attention. Poi translated as I shared the Best News in the World with the villagers. I asked if any would like to receive the gift of a life with God that Jesus purchased for them. A dozen raised their hands. They repeated after Poi as I led a prayer of salvation. The crowd was giddy with laughter, smiles, chatter, and anticipation.

Emily and Helen began triaging the patients, one at a time. Then it started to pour! A monsoon, whiting out the world outside. Still, the people lined up, waiting to be seen. As they waited, the nurses came by to ask them what problems they had. She would write the answers down on a card and then give it to me when I saw them. The wind started blowing and the rainwater started misting in underneath the roof on one side. We gathered the medicines and supplies and moved to the other side of the building to avoid the rain. Several times the wind would switch directions, the community hall full of people would pick up their plastic chairs and scramble to the other side of the hall, attempting to stay dry. People were excitedly squealing, laughing, and scrabbling back and forth, trying to dodge the wind and rain; it was like we were all on a ride at a waterpark.

Mark 9:38-41 NKJV:

> Now John answered Him, saying, "Teacher, we saw someone who does not follow us casting out demons in Your name, and we forbade him because he does not follow us."

> But Jesus said, "Do not forbid him, for no one who works a miracle in My name can soon afterward speak evil of Me. For he who is not against us is on our side. For whoever gives you a cup of water to drink in My name, because you belong to Christ, assuredly, I say to you, he will by no means lose his reward."

Possessed

This brings me back to the scene at the beginning of my story of Thailand, standing under a tin roof in a monsoon downpour, praying in tongues, English, and Thai, to help the lady who was possessed and unresponsive.

We prayed every Scripture as they came to mind, while the rain came down in sheets outside the community center.

Demons Cast out in Jesus' Name

After the woman's eyes opened, she remained seated in the chair, surrounded by our group and the village people. A few women were glaring at the woman, shaking their heads and talking obnoxiously loudly. They were not very sympathetic to her and were being quite rude about having to wait. I was wearing my white lab jacket and am six feet tall, which isn't unusually tall in the United States, but there I was at least a foot taller than any of the Akha locals. I looked at them and held my hand up. They got quiet, fast.

I asked the translator to tell the awakened woman to say "Hallelujah." The lady sitting in the chair quickly shook her head, no, and she didn't say anything. So we knew we weren't done yet. We started singing the same song again, "Jesus, Jesus, Jesus."

Many of the other villagers wanted us to just leave her alone. They said she would eventually get over it, since that was her pattern. Every time they had seen it, they just went on about their lives and ignored her. The clinic was interrupted, and several were annoyed but they were forced to stay as a captive audience and witness Jesus focusing on the needs of one woman, whom the village had given up on.

We continued singing the worship song until the woman told the translator that the demon had left her. I asked if she could say "Hallelujah," which she did. I asked if she could say "Jesus is King," and she did. Poi said the delivered woman was thanking us repeatedly. She sat quietly in the chair as we turned to resume the clinic. The intense rainstorm stopped as suddenly as it had started. The lack of rain hammering on the tin roof made the moment even more peaceful.

Convinced

By that time, it had gotten dark outside, and there were no lights in the community center. We got out four small flashlights to examine the people we were treating, read the cards, and look for medicine in the duffel bag. After that deliverance, the first people I treated were several elderly men who looked quite distinguished and reserved. They were the Akha tribal leaders.

I told Poi I didn't want to repeat the long invitation for salvation. I asked the translators to simply ask if they wanted to accept Jesus. The men forcefully nodded their heads up and down and said, "Yes," in Akha. They had just witnessed Jesus deliver that lady from the Akha spirits that had possessed her for years, without any other help or hope. They were convinced. I didn't have to give them any of the credentials of Christ.

After that, others prayed, asking Jesus into their hearts as we treated them one at a time. It was interesting how easy it was after they saw the power of Christ firsthand. We stayed for three more hours, treating the remaining 40 people. As we started packing our supplies, Helen Meyers came over to speak to me.

Praying for Leaders

Helen told me we needed to pray over three people because God was going to raise them up to be spiritual leaders in the community. The three were the mother and daughter Akha ladies who had helped Poi translate to Akha, and Joshua, the American husband of the daughter. They were already Christians and had already accepted Jesus into their lives. We prayed over them.

Joshua, the daughter's husband, was a tall, handsome, 26-year-old from Colorado who was living in the village with his wife and their kids. Joshua was raised by parents who were missionaries to Thailand. He had been in Thailand for five years, teaching at an international school. He was invited to a battered women's shelter as an example of a man they can trust, to show that they don't have to be afraid of all men. He met his wife, who had a child already, at the shelter. He told us she was pregnant with their first child together.

Joshua gave up all the benefits we have in the United States to live in this remote village, which was even more primitive than the town just 20 minutes down the road. There, most homes were cement block houses. He did it simply because he felt called to be there by God. Praying over Joshua, his wife, and her mother was our last act that night underneath that tin roof.

Money Is Not the Answer

1 Timothy 6:9-11 NKJV:

> But those who desire to be rich fall into temptation and a snare, and into many foolish and harmful lusts which drown men in destruction and perdition. For the love of money is a root of all kinds of evil, for which some have strayed from the faith in their greediness, and pierced themselves through with many sorrows.

> But you, O man of God, flee these things and pursue righteousness, godliness, faith, love, patience, gentleness.

Back at our hotel the next morning, during breakfast I was sitting with Nancy, the Chinese translator from the province of China that's right across from Hong Kong. Because it's right across from Hong Kong, it is freer about speech and trade than other parts of China. They hadn't yet seen the same level of persecution that other provinces were suffering.

She told me that, four years ago, she was invited by Pastor Paul, a pastor from Taiwan who ran Christian drug rehab ministries in Thailand. Two years later, she had come to Thailand again with our group. Before she came on this trip, they were asking for more money; money for the orphans, for the poor, for the ministry, and for buildings. She told them they didn't need more money. She already gave them money—what people needed was Jesus. She said she'd noticed that often, the Chinese pastors focused on money to meet the practical needs.

I took what she said as a very profound insight from her perspective. I considered that, because the Chinese people had come from a great lack and have suffered for generations because of that lack, they have seen many needs for healthcare, food, and clothing solved by money. The Christian leaders of these ministries were looking to meet the physical needs of all these people, so they were constantly begging for more money instead of focusing on prayer, spirituality, or Jesus. That was the frustration Nancy was expressing to me.

Later, we were all in the van and I mentioned Nancy's insights to Shanda. She said that she sees it in black people too. She told me that because the Chinese have been poor for so long, they think money is what they need. I figured that really any group that experienced a severe lack for an extended period will start to focus on money as a fix-all solution. Nancy called it a deception and said she thought the Christian leaders were deceived into thinking they needed money when their true need was for Jesus. It was interesting to hear all this from a Chinese lady from communist China, and to have a black lady from the United States agree. The devil will remind people of their past lack to put them in fear and make them want to seek tangible solutions to their problems, instead of spiritual ones.

Global Sex Trafficking

As I have mentioned, Thailand is a hub for sex trafficking. It is where some of the worst of the worst happens. Marcus Neal, a policeman from New Jersey, was a member of the mission team. He had a desire in his heart for years to rescue women and children from sex trafficking. When we went to the red-light district, he made connections with ministries rescuing trafficking victims.

Accursed Jewelry

We also visited a Christian school for the hill tribe people. The children were raised in Buddhist households, but then they were taught about Jesus and many of them became Christians. The parents of the children would also sometimes become Christians as well, because they were interested in why someone would help their children. We did a medical clinic at the children's preschool. Helen Todd shared the Good News with 20 children who accepted Jesus, and afterward they played games, sang songs, and heard a message. I ran the clinic where I noticed that there was one boy who had a Buddhist amulet around his neck. I asked him if it was okay if we took it off and he agreed, so we put it in his backpack. Once the necklace was removed, he seemed to pay more attention and was able to understand when I shared the Gospel. Then he wanted to accept Jesus, so we led him in a prayer of salvation.

Opium King's Lair to Christian Drug Rehab

We went to a drug rehab center in northern Thailand. There is a lot of drug use in Thailand, especially in that area of the country. It was expected there that every man would be a farmer, and that he would likely start using drugs. If you do use drugs, then you eventually start trafficking to support your habit, just like in the United States. Also, while prostitution is illegal there, they do have a red-light district, so you know they accept that sexual immorality.

Prostitution and drug use are officially against the law, but the laws are not enforced, for the most part. Even though they had police at the checkpoints, it seemed they were just waving everybody through. The security people were only there because they were told to be there.

We were told that most of the drug rehab programs in Thailand are run by Buddhist monks and are financially supported by the government. However, the place we went to was established in 1982 by Christians out of Taiwan and was not government supported. The building used to be the headquarters of the Opium King. The Opium King was famous, back in the day, when he was the numero uno of the drug trade. On the way in, we were taking a windy, one-lane mud road on the edge of a mountainside. We were in white minivans and it felt like we were just hanging on the slippery edge of that wall. I prayed the whole way that we wouldn't slide off into the valley below. At the entrance of the compound, we passed a big stone statue of the Opium King on a horse.

What was one of the world's major drug headquarters in the 50s is now used for a Christian drug rehab program. It was not like drug rehab in the United States; there wasn't really counseling, and they didn't have any medications. It's free for anyone to go there and each patient was given a Bible. In contrast, addicts have to pay to go to the government-funded drug rehab centers run by the Buddhist monks. I found great satisfaction in knowing the place where Christ set people free was free for them to access.

Drugs Make People Lazy

The only catch at this rehab facility was that people had to commit to staying there for a year and a half, without leaving the facility, and to have a role in taking care of their own needs. They farmed to grow their food and they fixed the roads in the area.

The philosophy is that drug users become lazy, so part of the program is hard work, along with Bible study and prayer. They'd get up at 5 a.m. for prayer time, then they'd do a full day of Bible study until 4 p.m. That was when they would start working in the fields or building roads. They'd do hard work until 9 p.m. at night. They couldn't leave, but their family could visit. That was the atmosphere people lived with for a year and a half, in order to recover from lives of drug abuse. The Christian workers there were committed. I could see the intensity in them; they were not there to play.

Beauty for Ashes

When most people got to the rehab center, their lives were ruined, their health was ruined, and they had no money or possessions. Then they would hear the Gospel of Jesus Christ and become disciples. There were two separate areas of the compound, creating a men's center and a women's center. There were also the children of some of the drug addicts living there, recovering. The children were bussed to the public school during the day, if they were citizens of Thailand.

233

Destined to Fail

We saw how it was there; if you were growing up as a man in that part of the world, you would most likely end up a drug user and, eventually, be in the drug trade. There were people there from Laos and Myanmar, the different hill tribes, Thai people, and the Chinese descendants of the Shan Kai-shek army, who fought against the communists in China and lost. These Chinese descendants of soldiers who fought Communism were people without citizenship to any nation. It was a real mix of people, but they all had three things in common: they were all raised in a corrupt spiritual atmosphere, they had all gotten hooked on drugs, and they all wanted to change their lives.

The whole program was about reading the Bible: Bible study and hard work. They had a high success rate of people staying the whole year and a half, and then many of them asked to stay for another two or four years, to be disciples. They wanted to be used as workers and teachers there, or to go out as missionaries or pastors. Most of them were not Christians when they came, but by the time we met them, all except for two of them were Christians. We prayed for the two people who were not Christians. They were fairly new to the drug rehab center and accepted Christ while we were there.

If You Only Had One Request

I did the medical clinic for the drug rehab men and met people from all of those different backgrounds. It was fascinating to me. The youngest person in rehab was only six years old. The oldest person I saw, and I don't know exactly how old he was, had been a Thai soldier and was missing a leg because he had stepped on a landmine when they were fighting communists back in the 50s. He was a frail old man with a low-budget prosthesis on his left leg. It didn't bend at the knee, but it was flesh colored. When I looked at the bottom of it, I just thought it was his leg.

Helen Todd asked him if there was anything we could pray for that he needed. Of course, he had nothing so he needed everything.

The one thing that he asked us to pray for was not money or food. He did not ask for a house, or a spouse, or any of those worldly things; he asked that we would pray that his faith would be stronger. Many of the patients at the rehab suffered from chronic anxiety and panic attacks; these are common ailments left over from past drug use.

We prayed for them, and they were smiling and laughing. They had new looks on their faces; it was clear to me that they were not the same. I believe that God was honoring their prayers, and their willingness to show up and not leave, to pray and to trust God. To ask even though they had asked many times before. I even got a big bear hug from one of them, who came back later to thank me again and again. Jesus is the one who helps people.

Luke 12:22-34 NIV

Then Jesus said to his disciples: "Therefore I tell you, do not worry about your life, what you will eat; or about your body, what you will wear. For life is more than food, and the body more than clothes. Consider the ravens: They do not sow or reap, they have no storeroom or barn; yet God feeds them. And how much more valuable you are than birds! Who of you by worrying can add a single hour to your life? Since you cannot do this very little thing, why do you worry about the rest?

"Consider how the wild flowers grow. They do not labor or spin. Yet I tell you, not even Solomon in all his splendor was dressed like one of these. If that is how God clothes the grass of the field, which is here today, and tomorrow is thrown into the fire, how much more will he clothe you—you of little faith! And do not set your heart on what you will eat or drink; do not worry about it. For the pagan world runs after all such things, and your Father knows that you need them. But seek his kingdom, and these things will be given to you as well.

"Do not be afraid, little flock, for your Father has been pleased to give you the kingdom. Sell your possessions and give to the poor. Provide purses for yourselves that will not wear out, a treasure in heaven that will never fail, where no thief comes near and no moth destroys. For where your treasure is, there your heart will be also.

The Golden Triangle

While we were in Chiang Rai, we visited the Golden Triangle, which was very close. We drove about 30 minutes down the highway to the actual Golden Triangle, where three countries meet: Myanmar, Laos, and Thailand. We had to go through a police checkpoint, and then it almost seemed, by the signs, that there had been a little town or village there. We went to the very epicenter, where the Ruak and Mekong rivers come together.

There we were, on the top of a mountain, standing beneath a huge idol of Buddha, able to look down at these rivers marking the borders of three countries. I looked across the river to Laos, where there is another huge, four-story Buddha statue mounted among the trees. Then I looked over at Myanmar and it just looked like jungle. There were some very oriental-looking boats going up and down the river.

We had a postcard view, despite the looming Buddhas. There were also huge statues of three-headed serpents on either side of the walkway. Each one was about 100 feet long, made out of stone. We were definitely in a very significant place for the Buddhist and Hindu people.

The Sign of Rain

There was a lot of spiritual activity throughout the area. We were there, both praying and acting like tourists. I bought a few shirts from a little open-air gift shop there. I've seen, sometimes, that God will give a sign when something's about to happen, like a rain shower hitting from out of the blue. Well, as soon as we were done praying and I walked into the gift shop, it started raining cats and dogs. We all got soaked running back to the vans. We were still praying that the people there would be freed from drug trafficking, human trafficking, murder, and all of the terrible things that go with those activities. We prayed this would become known as a place where Christ was promoted.

Jesus Still Heals

Our last day in Thailand was a Sunday, so we went to a local church service. During the church service, I stood up and told them about James Chapter 5, which says that anointing people with oil, a prayer of faith, and laying on hands can heal people. I also told them about Mark 16: 17-18, which describes believers laying hands on the sick and the sick will recover. I told them about my 8-year-old son in Argentina. He'd touched a lady on her forehead during prayer and she fell back in her chair. Afterward she'd said she felt fire hit the top of her head and go down her body into her right hip, where she had been in excruciating pain for months without any relief, and immediately the pain was gone. I told them I am a doctor, but I won't be here tomorrow, or next week, and their family and friends will eventually get sick. I told them to listen to what God says to do. I had an 8-year-old boy from the congregation come up to the front with me, so they could all see a clear picture of how God can use anybody at any age.

After the service we held a medical clinic on the porch of the church. I had the goal of dispersing the rest of my medicine. We were flying out that night and I still had many bottles of vitamins. Well, not only did we start treating the people who were in the church building, but it didn't take long for people from the village to show up as well. Soon we started running out of medicines and we still had a lot of people waiting be seen. We started praying.

One man was motioning with his hands. He could barely move the fingertips on one hand. Using his other hand, he was trying force the fingers to bend into a fist. He could barely move the fingertips at all. He was wincing and said it had been like that for months. We started praying for him and I felt led to tell him to grab my fingers with his hand.

He was barely able to close his hand a little bit around my fingers. I was praying, and moving his hand around, and praying. After about five minutes, his hand was opening and closing; he had a strong grip and was pain-free and happy.

Then I saw several people with knee pain and we prayed with them. I told them the Bible says faith without works is dead, but faith with works is alive, so do something. I told them to bend their knees with me, so we were doing squats while we were praying. I asked if the pain was gone, and they said it wasn't gone, but it was a lot less. So, we kept at the prayer and slow, careful squats until they were completely pain-free.

Then we saw a lady who, for three months, hadn't been able to use her shoulder. It was so stiff she could barely move it away from her body. We prayed for her shoulder, prayed for the ligaments and the rotator cuff, rebuking the inflammation and the pain, just like Jesus rebuked the fever in Peter's mother-in-law. We asked her to move her arm around as much as she could. I stood in front of her and started flinging my arms up into the air in front of me, saying, "Hallelujah." I told her to do that. She started doing it, and before we knew it, both arms were going all the way up and she was saying "Hallelujah!" She was excited and happy.

When I ran out of medicine, we still had a line of waiting patients. We prayed with each patient, and God healed people. I was satisfied that I passed out all of the medicine. We saw many healed by the Lord. Many accepted Christ as their savior. We had an evening of souvenir shopping before we flew from Chiang Rai to Bangkok.

Headed Home

At the Bangkok airport, we had to get on an hour-long shuttle bus to another airport where we could board our international flights. We had to wait until midnight for what was the last bus until 5 a.m. If we had missed that last shuttle, it would have been a disaster for a lot of our team, so we needed to make sure we all got on that bus. Waiting at the shuttle stop, I noticed a Caucasian man with a ponytail and a backpack.

Flag patches from Vietnam, Laos, Cambodia, and many other Asian countries were on his backpack. He looked like a Bohemian kind of dude. He said he was from Chicago originally, and he was waiting for the shuttle to the international airport as well. It ended up that he was the only other person on the bus with our team of missionaries and he was not a Christian. Once we got on the bus, I sat by him. I started telling him about the miracles I'd seen, and the Best News in the World. He had a book that he was acting like he was trying to read, but he listened and thanked me for telling him my stories. I asked if he was ready to accept the gift of Christ, but he said no.

Traveler's Story

His story was that he bought the cheapest flight he could to Asia: $300 for a flight from Chicago to Vietnam. He bounced around from place to place, doing jobs like bartending or leading tours. I told him he has seen pretty much everything that lifestyle has to offer, probably 10 times, and it was just not appealing anymore. I said I didn't want him to have second-best in life. I started telling him Nancy's story of how she became a Christian. I got about five minutes into the story before I yelled for Nancy to come trade places with me. For the rest of the trip, Nancy sat next to him, giving her testimony and telling him about Jesus until we pulled up to the airport. So, for the full 60 minutes we had together, he was totally immersed.

These realizations were going to wreck his current lifestyle. He would have to come up with a new, more wholesome way to survive in Asia. He had never considered any other way. I think that was part of the fear that stopped him. He thanked us for speaking with him but said he needed time to process the information.

Testify in the Sky

During the flight from Bangkok to Tokyo, I was seated next to a husband and wife from Jordan. It didn't take long for him to mention that he was agnostic, despite being from a predominantly Muslim country. He was a doctor on his way to do a pediatric residency in New York.

He had been providing medical care at the Syrian refugee camps in Jordan. Many of the refugees are children. That was why he decided to do a pediatric residency; so he could better care for children in need. I told him I was the medical director of an emergency room, and also a Christian. I started telling him reports of my medical missions. While he and his wife were listening, I pointed out that, with other religions, you have to be good enough to pay for your mistakes. In Christianity, God loves people, so He sent Jesus to pay that price for us. We just have to accept it by faith.

I told them about the lady in Iraq who had manifested a demon possession, and how she was delivered in Jesus' name. I told them about three Muslim women I met in Lebanon, who had dreams of Jesus talking to them and saw miracles happen right after the fact. I told them about my wife and me receiving a prophesy that the Lord said we would have a birth son, after we already had six adopted children. After being married 20 years, my wife turned 40 and became pregnant with our youngest son. I told them there are things that can't be explained by science, that medicine doesn't have to be the answer for everything. He said that's why we need research, but I told him that even with research, people are eventually going to die, so medicine isn't the answer for everything. We had a peaceful exchange of ideas.

The Lost Are Found

Texas

At 2 a.m., two weeks after returning from Thailand, I was taking care of a 2-year-old who had pneumonia. The oxygen saturation was low and the X-ray looked terrible. I walked past the TV monitor in the nurse's station. CBS was showing breaking news from Chiang Rai, Thailand. The whole world was talking about the lost children being found in

LOST BOYS OF THAILAND

Chiang Rai. A group of 12-year-old soccer players and their coach had left their bicycles at the entrance of a cave in Chiang Rai and did not come back out. They were missing for 10 days. Countries around the world joined an international effort to find those kids. The children were found after 10 days of wandering lost through this network of caves. They had ended up six miles deep in the caves and were trapped by floodwaters blocking their exit.

It was a sign that the lost are being found in Thailand, and the news was shaking the whole world. We had Christians from China, Taiwan, the United States, and Canada, all working in the small, never-reported-on province of Chiang Rai, Thailand. It was just like the little baby born in a manger 2,000 years ago. Most of the people of that generation did not recognize a Holy Sign for the whole human race. The Chiang Rai lost boys being found was a sign from God of the end-time harvest.

These types of events happen to confirm the time we are in right now. It's not an accident that the lost were 12-year-old boys, because Thailand is a hub of international sex trafficking and human trafficking. If you go to Google and type in "Thailand," it will take you about 10 seconds to come across the topic of trafficking. One disturbing trend in Thailand is "boy-girls." Wicked people make little boys cross-dress like transvestites before being molested. Thailand has been steeped in those horrors for centuries, but the rescuing of the Chiang Rai lost is a sign of what God is doing to rescue the poor and desperate. Things have been especially dark for the forgotten in the north of Thailand, which is where the Golden Triangle is. The people there have never had any attention on the world stage and now they are the focus of the BBC, CBS, NBC, CNN, and more.

That was also the first time ever that the World Missions Alliance sent a team to Thailand. The north is where the poorest of the poor are in Thailand. Those people are forgotten. They are not considered citizens of Thailand, and they are some of the most desperate people on earth. For them to get noticed by the world is amazing. God is in the details; He is using those kids to speak to the people of the world. Clearly the whole situation is a sign that God is going to the people who have been overlooked by the world and highlighting them (Luke 14:21). He put the global spotlight on those who have been forgotten. When the rescue was in process, the whole world could not get enough information about them. Jesus said, in the last days, servants would be sent out to invite people into the marriage supper of the Lamb. They would be sent to the highways and byways; to those who were outcast and forgotten. God has made me his servant and allowed me to share these messages with you, now.

After returning home, I found a *The Jakarta Post* article dated March 10, 2018: "Vietnamese contestant crowned queen in Thai transgender pageant" (https://www.thejakartapost.com/life/2018/03/10/viet-namese-contestant-crowned-queen-in-thai-transgender-pageant.html). All contestants were men given female estrogen hormones, nose jobs, and plastic surgery to produce a feminine appearance. They were all dressed as women and competed in an international beauty contest. A contestant judge was quoted as saying that only in Thailand could such a pageant be held. He clearly thought that was a good thing. That story expressed the "anything goes, total abandonment of boundaries and norms" in the natural dimension, which we sensed in the supernatural dimension.

Dated July 14, 2018, a *BBC News* article was titled, "The full story of Thailand's extraordinary cave rescue" (https://www.bbc.com/news/world-asia-44791998). The article said on June 23, 2018, a soccer team of 12 hill tribe boys and their coach explored a cave after soccer practice. Rain waters flooded the cave behind them and they were trapped. An international effort including U.S. Air Force rescue specialists, cave divers from the U.K., Belgium, Australia, and Scandinavia, and Thai Navy SEALs searched and found the kids.

Until this event, the people of Chiang Rai were unnoticed by the world. Hill tribe children who had been overlooked by the world were thrust in the spotlight of worldwide coverage. Until this event, the undervalued hill tribe boys were destined to be abused by people from around the world. After the news coverage, the same boys were now greatly valued and worldwide prayers were raised for the lost to be found and saved. Not only were they found, but all were saved alive by the international rescue effort. That happened in the same small town, Chiang Rai, where we had just witnessed a spiritual parallel event. Our international team found spiritually lost people who were saved by accepting Jesus as their Lord and Savior.

Many of the people of Thailand have been living a cursed life. The Holy Spirit says that "all the blessings of Abraham are yes and amen through Christ our savior." One blessing is "You are the head and not the tail, above and never beneath, blessed in the city, blessed in the field, blessed coming in, blessed going out, everything you put your hand to will prosper, you will lend to many and borrow from none." Most of the Thai who are not in relationship with Jesus (Yeshua as he is known in the much of the world), do not have evidence of that blessing. In fact, they are "the tail, below and never above, cursed in the field and city . . ."

BBC News, on May 21, 2019, published a story of sorrow: "Germany sex trafficking: Thai forced prostitution trial begins" (https://www.bbc.com/news/world-europe-48350961). Over 200 Thai women and children had their passports confiscated and salaries withheld, and were forced to rotate through a network of brothels in Germany. Four Thai women and one German man have been arrested so far. Not only are the Thai used and abused by people of other nations in Thailand, but they are abused and used internationally. That is why the Holy Spirit is prompting so many to share the Good News in Thailand so the Thai can be set free via a relationship with Christ.

Also on my return home, I learned that the medical board had considered all three letters they received about my case (mine, the ENT's—Dr. Cepero—and the recanting letter from the pediatrician who filed the complaint) and had decided to dismiss the complaint. I was cleared of any wrongdoing. I am so grateful that we have an Advocate with the Father (1 John 2:1).

Letters Concerning Texas Medical Board Complaint

Baraa Alabd Alrazzak, M.D.
6431 Fannin St.
MSB 3 137
Houston, TX 77030

May 30, 2018

<u>VIA HAND DELIVERY</u>
Texas Medical Board
P.O. Box 2018 MC-263
Austin, TX 78768-2018

    Re: Richard Paul Bartlett, M.D.
           File #: 18-6341

To whom it may concern:

I am a pediatric hospitalist and the complainant in the above-referenced matter. I filed the complaint against Dr. Bartlett after an incident involving the transfer of a one year old patient who was suspected of having epiglottitis. I primarily work in Houston but occasionally cover the Medical Center Hospital in Odessa. I was in Odessa on the day in issue. It was my feeling at the time that Dr. Bartlett, the ER physician at Excel ER in Odessa, Texas, had misrepresented facts to me during our transfer discussions. I filed this complaint in haste, the same evening, before I had all of the facts and a full understanding of the circumstances. Dr. Bartlett was trying to transfer the patient from his facility to the Medical Center Hospital here in Odessa. As I work in Odessa periodically, I did not know that Dr. Bartlett did not have the availability of a helicopter to transfer this patient to Lubbock for a center with a higher level of care where there was a pedi-ICU. The patient was ultimately transferred to my service through the ER at Medical Center Hospital here in Odessa. He was operated immediately on by Dr. Cepero and has done well overall.

I think that all of the physicians involved acted appropriately and certainly had this patient's best interests at heart. With a full understanding of the circumstances, I now do not feel that this complaint should be pursued. In retrospect, I wish I had not filed it. I called the TMB on 5/25/18 in an attempt to retract it but was told that I was not able to. I am writing this letter in hopes that the complaint will simply be dismissed.

Sincerely,

Baraa Alabd Alrazzak, M.D.

Recanting letter from Dr. Alrazzak, the original complainant.

Ralph Cepero, M.D.
540 West 5th Street, Suite 410
Odessa, TX 79731

June 5, 2018

VIA HAND DELIVERY
Texas Medical Board
P.O. Box 2018 MC-263
Austin, TX 78768-2018
    Re: Richard Paul Bartlett, M.D.
       File #: 18-6341

Dear Members of the Medical Board,

I am writing this letter in response to a complaint that has been filed against Dr. Richard Paul Bartlett, who works in the Excel ER in Odessa, Texas. I know Dr. Bartlett professionally and have had reason to consult with him on many occasions. I find him to be a very fine physician who is of the utmost character. I am an ENT and work at Medical Center Hospital ("MCH") in Odessa, Texas. I was involved in the transfer discussions regarding ███████████ at issue and can assure this Board that Dr. Bartlett did not make any misrepresentations to me in discussing this patient.

Specifically, on 5/13/18, Dr. Bartlett called me and told me that he had a 1 year old patient who had presented to his freestanding ER. He believed that the patient had early, acute epiglottitis. He gave me the patient's vital signs, physical findings and x-ray findings and advised me that the patient was stable at the time. Dr. Bartlett felt that ██████ needed a higher level of care where he could be operated on if necessary and I agreed with that assessment. We discussed the various transfer options and the timing of same. I agreed to examine the patient and if necessary, take him to the OR. However, I asked Dr. Bartlett to contact the pediatric hospitalist to medically manage the patient if necessary. It is my understanding that he spoke with Dr. Alrazzak, who is a pediatric hospitalist who primarily works in Houston but covers MCH occasionally. I was not privy to the conversation between Dr. Bartlett and Dr. Alrazzak. Dr. Alrazzak told me that he regretted filing the complaint in haste and tried to take it back. Dr. Alrazzak has written a letter advising the Board that Dr. Bartlett did not make any misrepresentations as he had once believed.

Importantly, ██████ was transferred to MCH where I evaluated him, took him to the OR and discovered laryngeal edema but the child did not require ICU monitoring.

I believe that all of the physicians involved in ██████ care were acting with his best interest at heart. I applaud Dr. Bartlett for his astute examination and diagnosis of ██████ and his quick action on his behalf. This patient had a good outcome due in large part to Dr. Bartlett's thoughtful care. I hope that this is helpful and hope that this matter can be dismissed.

Sincerely,

Ralph Cepero, M.D.

Letter 2 from Ralph Cepero, M.D., supporting Dr. Bartlett's actions.

Photos Taken for Thailand Mission

Rattlesnake trapped by closing clinic door.

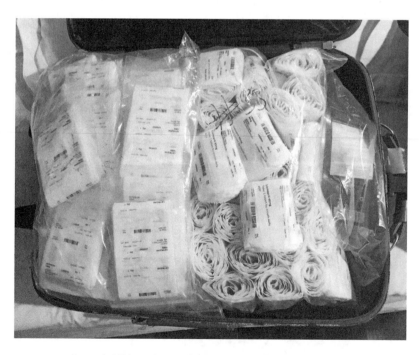

Smuggled life-saving medicines in luggage on Thailand trip.

Bangkok idols in airport.

Hill tribe women waiting for clinic.

Lesions from hill tribe tradition of "coining" for sore throat.

Hill tribe women in Thailand.

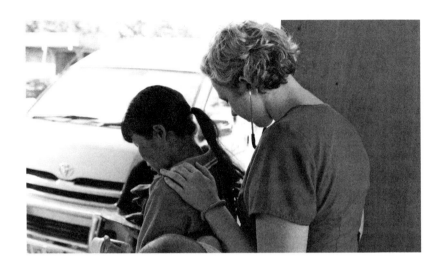

Nurse Emily examines a hill tribe woman during a health clinic in Thailand.

Dr. Bartlett examines an Akha woman delivered from demon possession in Thailand.

The stairway at the Golden Triangle in Thailand.

CHAPTER 8

Serbia, Gypsies, and God

Serbia in the News

BBC News published an article on March 20, 2019, titled "Radovan Karadzic sentence increased to life at U.N. Tribunal" (https://www. bbc.com/news/world-europe-47642327). The article was about the Bosnian Serb former leader who was involved in the Bosnian civil war and was found guilty, in 2016, of genocide and war crimes by the U.N. tribunal in The Hague. At that time, he was given a 40-year sentence, so he appealed the sentence and they decided at the appeal hearing that the sentence was too light and he should get life without parole. It was not a good idea for him to appeal it. The article mentioned that he was a psychiatrist before he became a dictator.

Karadzic was mentioned in another story published on March 15, 2019. That *BBC News* article was called "New Zealand mosque shooting: What is known about the suspect?" (https://www.bbc.com/news/world-asia-47579243). The article described the terrorist who went into several mosques and killed 50 people. The terrorist was videoing himself with a head-mounted camera setup to livestream the attack. He was playing a song that praised the Serb leader, Radovan Karadzic. He also was playing the anthem of the Serbian paramilitary. That was all in the news prior to my trip to Serbia.

Drug Rehab: Jesus Gives Another Chance at Life

June 17, 2019

We flew into Belgrade, Serbia. Pastor Beredi Dusan (Bera) gave us a ride north to Novi Sad. We passed extensive fields of abundant crops. Pastor Bera explained that the soil is fertile and the climate ideal for agriculture. Many of the Caesars of the Roman empire were born in Serbia or moved to Serbia for that reason. Bera explained that foreign investors from Saudi Arabia owned vast farms in Serbia. Novi Sad is translated to "new garden." Originally, Bera started a Teen Challenge Drug Rehab program in Novi Sad. Heroine is cheap and plentiful, and the poor economy and oppression of the corrupt government was a breeding ground for hopelessness. Bera broke away from Teen Challenge with his own model of a rehab program.

Later, he was led to start a church with his wife, the Protestant Christian Fellowship. Cheap property in the middle of town was bought. The government invested in an urban renewal project and large, expensive new properties were built around their church in the middle of downtown. The property value of the church, which had been paid for, skyrocketed. They are strategically located in the center of a large population that is growing. Most of the initial congregants were recovering or former addicts. Now many first-time attendees are joining and many are being discipled. One of the recovered addicts became the director of the rehab program. Another established a ministry to all homeless people in Novi Sad. The church is the largest evangelical church in all of Serbia, with several hundred members.

Homeless Ministry: Luke 14:21

Our mission coincided with the timing for the homeless ministry. We set up a medical clinic in the sanctuary. The walls and doors were anointed as the mission team prayed throughout the room and commanded all unclean spirits to leave. My wife, Dawn, played the keyboard and my

10-year-old son Grant played the violin. Worship music was played during the entire clinic.

Prior to serving the homeless, Pastors Danijel and Vera Kuranji brought their 26-year-old son to the clinic for help. His name is Filip. At 8 months old, he had adenocarcinoma in one kidney and Wilm's tumor in the other, as a result of Chernobyl. Amazingly, he survived the surgeries and cancer. He married, but with insulin diabetes and a frozen shoulder, he felt hopeless and defeated. We anointed Filip and prayed that his shoulder would be healed. We prayed that he would live to see his grandchildren.

Mirko Bakocervic serves as pastor of a satellite church in a neighboring town. Mirko was standing on the periphery. While praying for Filip, Mirko felt a series of pops in his back. He had suffered with chronic back pain for years and was instantly healed. Mirko left in a hurry to gather his wife, Mirjana, and kids Ethan and Emily, and bring them to the church. Mirjana suffered with headaches from a brain tumor. We anointed Mirjana and prayed that she would see her grandchildren. She stayed to pray with us for others that morning.

One by one, all 20 of the men in the heroine rehab program came through the clinic for care and prayer. One of those men, Nenad Marcetic, had been a truck driver all over Europe for 20 years. I delivered a prophecy to Nenad that he would be a Godly mentor used by the Lord to help many men.

Andjelko Trninic Gale was the youth pastor. He was a newlywed and did freelance photography. He helped translate.

Many of the homeless men and women had untreated hypertension and diabetes. I washed each patient's feet as I prayed for them. I had a new experience of Mark 16, which says, "Believers will lay hands on the sick." Some were initially embarrassed and resisted, but all eventually allowed me to wash their feet. Many feet stank and had severe fungal infections. All understood that it was a spiritual act. Many of the homeless were highly educated—engineers and former professors. A diabetic in a wheelchair with one calloused, rough, and dirty foot was moved by the experience. I understood that Jesus wanted to show honor, love, and respect for the unloved. Another man who had a recent toe amputation had his neglected, dirty, crusty feet washed. Jesus wanted them to feel His compassion. Believers are the tangible hands of Jesus. During the clinic, medication was given when indicated.

JoAnn Wolfe, R.N., brought a variety of reading glasses. Those in need tried various glasses until their faces would light up with joy. Each was as excited as a child during Christmas to receive the gift of improved sight.

A former soldier in the war against NATO and the U.S., 20 years prior, came for care. He was a gentle and honorable man, homeless because of the political and economic hardship of Serbia. It was an honor to wash his feet. A homeless engineer explained that he worked every odd job he could find to put his daughter through college and graduate school. She could not find employment because the economy was so bad. He did not regret investing in his daughter's education despite his homeless state.

The pastor of the Homeless Ministry was healed of hepatitis C with the Pegasus medication. He was reinfected after he relapsed and used IV heroine again. He is now happily married, clean, and sober with a 6-year-old daughter. He and his wife pick up all the homeless they can find every two weeks and bring them to the church. A hot meal is served. A barber gives free shaves and haircuts. Hot showers are provided.

Migrants: Moved to Hear the Good News

News reports of waves of illegal migrants streaming into Western Europe were increasing. A hired driver with a van took Chuck Todd, JoAnn Wolfe, R.N., Kendall Petty, R.N., Kathy Santen, Theresa Harris, and Linda Smith north from Novi Sad to Subotica, Serbia. A Serbian pastor named Varga Tibor had been providing blankets and food and sharing the Good News of Jesus with migrants for years.

SERBIA, GYPSIES, AND GOD

We arrived after several hours of highway travel to Subotica. It was dreary and overcast as we pulled up to Tibor's house that Sunday morning. Tibor helped transfer the medical supplies into the back of his van. In his yard, left in the rain, was the soaked back seat for the van. We carried it to the van and secured it in place. JoAnn Wolfe pulled a new tarp, still in the plastic packaging, out of her backpack. She said she knew it was strange but she knew she should bring it. Evidence again that God does speak to his people. God is in the details.

All had dry seats in the van as Tibor drove to an abandoned train station outside of town. He came there often over the years to show kindness to the migrants. Tibor explained that the migrants are transient. Often the people are not there the next day. Many brick and block two-story buildings with all windows broken out and doors removed surrounded several sets of rail tracks. No evidence of people was visible. The ladies on the team stayed in the van with the medical supplies. Tibor, Chuck, and I walked through tall weeds and puddles to the first building. Tibor walked into the first building and found a group of Middle Eastern young men. They had heard of the Iranian who Tibor asked about but had not seen him. When asked, they said they needed no medical help. We looked in several other buildings. There was no electricity or running water or plumbing. Trash was strewn throughout, along with several filthy buckets for water and small blankets, all the same size and navy blue. Tibor said those were donated.

In some buildings we found blankets neatly folded, with the concrete floors swept and buckets empty, showing that someone was clearly trying to keep order. Other rooms and buildings were filthy with blankets discarded in the mud outside.

When we returned to the van, the ladies were talking to a lone young man. He explained he was from Iran. He had arrived with friends over a year before. After multiple attempts to illegally sneak across the Hungarian border, he was the only one left. He was an illegal migrant, without money, without food, with only the clothes on his back. Without his friends, he did not know where his next meal would come from. He expressed his hopelessness and cynical perspective. I shared the Good News of Jesus with him. He decided he would like to accept the gift that Jesus paid for. I led him in a prayer. His sour countenance turned to smiles and joy. We gave him some snacks, instant coffee, bottles of water, and first-aid supplies. As we loaded into the van, he repeatedly thanked us and was visibly hopeful and at peace.

Tibor drove into the countryside another 20 minutes toward the Hungarian border. Several abandoned co-op farm buildings were in fields of wet, tall weeds and grass surrounded by forest. It was noon and there was no evidence of humans in sight. The first small building had 13 young men from Mumbai, India, living in cramped, primitive squalor. Blankets and trash were strewn in several rooms where they slept on filthy concrete in the dark, windowless rooms. A small soot-stained room with remnants of a fire was for cooking the weeds, etc., that they foraged for food.

When asked, they all had the same medical need. Several bared their feet and ankles to show oozing, excoriated, red rashes of scabies and chiggers. We gave some medical attention and then asked the one migrant who spoke English to translate as I shared the Good News of Jesus. Seven immediately responded that they wanted to accept Jesus into their lives. In the dark room that was their bedroom, they repeated after the translator a prayer I led. They explained they were highly educated but were in search of better economic opportunity. They told us that a large group of young men from Pakistan and Afghanistan were in a large abandoned silo nearby. We drove the short distance and 13 young men came out of the building to meet us. Most studied us, keeping their distance. One came forward who spoke English. They too were eaten up with scabies and chiggers and all came closer in hopes of relief. Appropriate medication was doled out. Smiles and foreign chatter replaced silent suspicion. The back of the van was opened up. It provided shelter from a sudden downpour of rain. The migrants huddled tightly together under the van door.

I had the translator repeat my explanation of the Good News of Jesus. I explained that everyone makes mistakes. No one is perfect. God knew we would make mistakes. God loves us. God sent his only son, Jesus, who is perfect, to die and pay a price we could never pay, so we could have a gift of life with God forever. But it's like someone offering a present. It is not yours until you choose to accept it. I asked if any had heard that before. All indicated they had not. I asked if they would like to accept the gift of life Jesus paid for. Seven men in unison repeated the prayer I led as the translator spoke in their native tongue.

As suddenly as the rain had started, it ended after the prayer. The men stepped back from the van because the rain had stopped. I realized the rain forced the young men to press in, making eye contact with only myself. Their peers being out of line of sight decreased their fear of reprisal for asking Jesus into their hearts, asking for forgiveness, forgiving all, asking to be covered with the Holy Spirit, and asking Jesus to be in charge of their thoughts, words, and actions. Afterwards, several of the men gratefully accepted personal prayers offered by mission members through the translator. JoAnn Wolfe passed out the remaining packets of instant coffee and snacks. We loaded in the van and drove to a local village for lunch.

The Poor and Lame: Jesus Is the Healer

After lunch, Tibor invited us to an afternoon service at a small congregation he pastored. He picked up a couple with an infant sitting on the side of the highway on the way to the small church building in Cantavir, Serbia. We arrived early to the church building, so our small team went for a walk in the neighborhood. We arrived on a street that ended in a cemetery.

Looking at gravestones, I was surprised to see my grandmother's maiden name, Toth. Her parents were Hungarian immigrants to America. We returned to the church. The group of thirty congregants were led in worship songs by Tibor's teenage children, who played the keyboard, guitar, and drums. The congregants were poor, and many clearly had hard lives prior to joining the group. No one of affluence was present.

Tibor asked the couple to bring their baby forward for the scheduled baby dedication. He then asked our team to introduce ourselves to the congregation. I told them I had found the name Toth repeatedly in the local cemetery and that I may be related to them. Pastor Tibor laughed and said his wife's maiden name is Toth! God *is* in the details.

Afterward, Tibor asked if any were ill in the church and wanted prayer. An obese, elderly woman immediately rose from her seat, leaning on a crutch under her right arm. She explained that she had suffered severe left hip pain for 19 years. She had a right knee replacement in the past. Tibor invited me to pray for her. Following God's instruction in James 5, we anointed and prayed for her. She yelled that her pain was gone. I asked her to do something she could not do before. She twisted and stretched in all directions and shouted repeatedly because she was pain-free, with full range of motion. We started dancing in middle of the little modest room with many people cheering and praising the Lord. She continued to shout Hallelujahs with hugs and kisses for anyone within reach.

Her name was Simokovic Rozalia, although she was called Maria. Her parents were extremely poor Hungarians. She was sold as a bride at 9 years old to an older man and had suffered a difficult life. But now she could not contain her joy and love. Others had moved closer, hoping for prayer. She vigorously waved them closer, insisting they were helped. Lakatos Ibolya was another older woman who had suffered from pain in her arms and legs for four years. Nothing had relieved her pain. During prayer she excitedly reported the pain was gone. The congregation was praising the Lord even louder. Lakatos insisted that we pray for her son, Tangi. He was 22 years old and had just had an operation but was very ill, according to his mother. Tangi was not present but prayers were offered on his behalf.

Kovac Zsuzsa was an adult lady who had suffered with shoulder pain for four months. We laid hands on her and prayed. Zsuzsa exclaimed that her pain was gone. She held both hands high and repeatedly shouted "Hallelujah!" More worship, praise, and prayers ensued. We loaded in the van and Tibor offered to drive us the three-hour trip back to Novi Sad. He told us that the following week he was scheduled to go to a home to drive demons out from a young man and from the property. We prayed the young man would no longer be tormented.

Roma Village: Jesus Accepts the Social Outcasts

We went to a Roma village north of Novi Sad for two days. Roma are unwanted in every nation and not considered citizens with afforded privileges. The Roma culture is marked by murder, fortune-telling, witchcraft, theft, incest, and immorality of every sort. Historically, alcoholism and drug abuse have been rampant. Also, Roma children fend for themselves. It is unheard of for Roma children to receive any education. The Roma children, at 10 years old, join the adults in hard labor in the fields from sunrise to dark every day.

Sasha is a Roma who became a Christian. He then started a small church in a small home in the center of the village. He started a program in the tiny church to teach Roma children to read and write. All of the village children learn in the church.

Sasha is the trusted liaison between government aid and the Roma. The local government coordinates with Pastor Sasha to provide rudimentary medical care to the Roma. Children are brought by Sasha and the only other church leader, a young man who has the role of youth leader to the area Serbian medical clinic, when ill and for immunizations. Free meals are provided by church members to all elderly of the village. Efforts to meet basic needs of all in the village have caused many to join the church and caused changes in the local culture.

Prior to the church, Sasha said every other home in the village was a house of prostitution. At the time of our mission, only two remained.

Reports of positive change in the village caused Christians from other European nations to donate for the church. No evidence of extravagance was present in the one-room church building. Although it had electricity for lighting, no heating was evident. Despite the lack of indoor plumbing, the low ceiling, and cheap chairs and tables as furniture, the facility was a source of pride in the village. The youth pastor had a guitar, which was the lone instrument present.

Pastor Sasha said that despite the positive moral gains in the community, tragedy had occurred regularly. Fifty-six children had died in the last two years. Cancers, choking, asthma, and being struck by cars were most of the "natural" causes. We prayed that the children would be protected from further tragedy.

We returned the following evening for a medical clinic. Most the village worked in the fields from dawn to dark. We arrived at sunset. We anointed the walls, doors, and windows as we commanded all that is unclean to leave and asked for God to send angelic help.

The clinic was big news to the whole village. All were welcome. Roma started gathering outside the front door in the dark, waiting to come in. The elderly and women waited outside in plastic chairs. Inside, at one small table, Kendall Petty, R.N., and JoAnn Wolfe, R.N., triaged patients. Vital signs and medical history were obtained with the assistance of Sasha and the youth pastor translating. The patients would wait with their triage notes to be seen at another small table.

As it became dark outside, loud polka music started next door. Many of the Roma children have skin and hair signs consistent with vitamin deficiencies. All were given chewable multivitamins. Respiratory and ear infections were treated. Most of the children were happy and full of energy. When the Good News was presented, most of the children did not hesitate to respond that they were believers in Jesus and had Jesus in their hearts.

Not so for the adults. Almost every adult smoked. Many had wheezes and abnormal lung sounds. Kendall reached over from her table, handing me a triage paper. She said that the 40-year-old woman seated at her table has been diagnosed with lung cancer and her lungs sounded terrible. I waved her over to the empty chair ahead of other patients.

After reviewing the triage paper with her, I listened to her lungs. In 25 years of medical practice, I had never heard worse breathing sounds in both of her lungs—rales, wheezes, and rhonchi throughout. Kendall watched, shaking her head no slowly with a sorrowful expression.

Through the translator, I asked the woman if she liked good news. She nodded. I told her the Best News in the World. She said she had never heard the Gospel of Jesus before. When asked, she said she would like to accept the gift of life with God, which Jesus purchased. She repeated as I led her in a prayer. I then asked if we could pray for her health. We anointed her head with oil. I placed my hand on her back and the Roma youth pastor translated as I prayed.

He leaned toward me and said, "She says it burns when you touch her."

I kept praying, repenting of generational sins of her ancestors as they came to mind. I was also applying healing Scriptures to her health, rebuking cancer and various diseases in Jesus' name. She started to cough. As we prayed, the cough became more violent. Coughing gave way to choking. The distress worsened and she began to have trouble moving air. She was panicking, eyes darting around as she gasped. She was in respiratory distress. The village was 30 miles from the nearest town with medical services. No ambulance would come to this village even if called.

In my Texas ER, I would have ordered emergency IV meds, nebulizer treatments, and supplemental oxygen. I would have begun preparations to intubate. Of course, I was not in an equipped Texas ER; I was in a tiny, Roma one-room church in the middle of nowhere Serbia.

God had to intervene. I had seen Him help when there was no way things could end well. Suddenly she coughed and became calm. She then was clearly breathing freely. Her tense muscles visibly relaxed.

I stopped praying and picked up my stethoscope. I listened to the upper and lower lung fields of both lungs. I motioned for Kendall Petty to listen to her lungs. Kendall placed her stethoscope to the woman's back. Speechless, she slowly shook her head no as tears streamed down her cheeks.

Kendall looked at those gathered and whispered, "Her lungs are clear!" Loud Hallelujahs and cheering ensued. The woman opened the window and shouted into the night that Jesus had healed her. She walked to the front door. She again shouted to the dark neighborhood over the waiting patients that she was healed by Jesus.

Many waiting outside in the dark began speaking at the same time as she repeatedly told them that Jesus had healed her. Some waiting leaned toward her, reaching for her arm, and more questions prompted her to excitedly repeat what God had done. Pastor Sasha came from the door to say even more people were gathering in the dark outside, seeking care. He offered to send them away, concerned that we would wear out if we stayed late and then drove several hours back to Novi Sad. We decided that no one seeking help should be sent away.

A Roma woman who did manual labor in the fields suffered with chronic severe back pain. After the history and physical, medication was given. She too accepted Christ and afterward allowed us to pray for her health. She said her back felt much better. When pressed, she said that there was still discomfort but she felt much better. Smiling, she was content with the improvement. She left to stand by the door, talking to others.

Five minutes later, I asked Pastor Sasha to ask her if she still had pain. Yes, but she felt much better. I treated several patients and noticed she was still standing by the door talking to Sasha. I asked again how she felt. Better, but still some discomfort.

She left into the night. After treating more patients for 30 minutes, she came running through the door, excitedly speaking to Sasha. She said Jesus had totally healed her! Cheers and praise to God followed the report. I told her to tell the people waiting outside in the dark what God had done for her. She opened the door and shouted that Jesus healed her. She stayed outside surrounded by others hoping for help, explaining what God did for her.

Pastor Sasha had his blood pressure checked by JoAnn Wolfe. He felt fine. He used to take blood pressure medicine but ran out a long time ago. It was 210/110. I performed a physical exam and gave him a year's worth of medication. Sasha's blood pressure was rechecked, and was 154/94. He thanked us and continued to help by translating for other patients.

Although he had not taken meds, we rechecked his blood pressure 30 minutes later. At that point it was 120/80. Shouts of joy and praise to Jesus again streamed from the tiny one-room building throughout the village. We anointed Sasha and began to pray. Sasha swayed as if drunk. He was propped up by men surrounding him as he was covered in prayer. Prayers turned to prophecy that God was giving Sasha more favor with governments. Loud screeching and fighting of cats outside the window competed for attention during the prayers but subsided as the prayer ended.

A 20-year-old woman who had "an issue of blood" for over five years came for help. She was suicidal and overwhelmed. She was married at 12, divorced at 15, and shunned by family and the Roma community. She heard the Good News of Jesus for the first time and prayed to ask Jesus into her heart and to be in charge of her thoughts, words, and actions. She prayed for healing. We prayed for her health and repentance of specific iniquity by her ancestors as they came to mind. She was visibly strengthened and joyful.

A woman who appeared to be in her 70s complained of chronic aches and pains throughout her body. She was raising her granddaughter. She had been tormented with thoughts of suicide. She smoked and had a chronic cough and was exhausted. She heard the Good News for the first time and prayed to ask Jesus to be in charge of her life and heal her body. We prayed for her, including intercession of repentance for sins of hers and her ancestors for prostitution, witchcraft, theft, etc.

Her face transformed during prayer, looking decades younger. Pastor Warren Cook of San Antonio and I witnessed the transformation. She exclaimed her pains were gone and that she was healed by God. She too shouted out the window to the village that Jesus had healed her. As she left the building, she was surrounded by the curious and hopeful waiting in the cold dark night. Sasha quietly told me that the woman's daughter was in fact one of the last prostitutes in the village and the family had been heavily involved in witchcraft. We prayed that the daughter would receive Jesus and live in His freedom.

A Roma woman with many rings, necklaces, and a chain with a cross came for depression, cough, and general pain. I noted that several ungodly symbols were on the excessive jewelry. She had never been in the church before. She heard the Good News and prayed to ask forgiveness for her mistakes from God and accepted the gift of life with God that Jesus purchased for her.

Most of the adults were delivered during prayer from smoking and addictions that night. Sasha told us several days later that 20 confirmed healings during prayer occurred that night. Many who came to the church for medical help had never participated in church or been on the property before. Sasha said that many were being added to the church. Kendall Petty said she had been working as an oncology nurse for the last year. She had bonded to patients of all ages who were fighting cancer. She prayed for them but was heartbroken time and again as they passed away. She said she had hope and faith increased by the healings she witnessed.

Thoughts About Missions

Teamwork Makes the Dream Work

The Bible says that we are co-laborers with Christ. The Bible says we can do nothing of eternal value without Christ. God does not need a majority of natural soldiers to take the land. David had his mighty men; Jonathan worked with his armor bearer. Elijah had Elisha, Moses worked with Joshua, and Moses also partnered with Aaron. The pattern is clear in Scripture; two can withstand their enemy but their enemy can overcome one. A cord of three is not easily broken. God is the first cord and we are the second, and third, etc.

In contrast, there are plenty of examples in Scripture of men of God being overtaken when they are by themselves. When David let his army go to war while he stayed home alone, he fell. Samson was a loner and he was overcome. Many of the judges in the Book of Judges fell by themselves. Paul traveled with Luke, and Paul sometimes traveled with Mark and others. When Paul was by himself, he asked that someone be sent to help him. When two missionaries travel together, temptations to sin are minimized. Scripture instructs that we should give no occasion for the devil to attack.

Consider sniper teams; a sniper team includes the rifleman and a spotter. The spotter will calculate the distance and watch the over-all field of battle. That keeps the sniper from being surprised by an attack that he could not see coming because he was focused on the goal. Scripture also says that one can put 1,000 to flight, and two will put 10,000 to flight. The effect of two is multiplied in unity. Jesus said that "where two or more are gathered in my name, I am there in their midst." (Matthew 18:20)

God Is the Majority

In the spiritual dimension, God has, and is, the winning majority. Most of the time it does not look that way in the natural world. Elisha's servant had his eyes opened and saw God's many angels. Two-thirds of the angels did not rebel with Satan and chose to serve the Lord. Our victory is not by power, might, nor by finances, but by God's Holy Spirit. The Lord has ultimate power.

PDAs Are Good

The strategy is to tell the truth in love. Acts of love are necessary. The strategy is to use public displays of affection. Kudos to Crossroads Fellowship of Odessa, Texas. When my son and I went to Guatemala with Crossroads, we saw that Crossroads was excellent at loving people. On the same mission trip, mechanics were fixing vehicles for pastors and missionaries for free, others were building structures for the church, and yet others were providing medical care. On several trips, World Missions Alliance had a young lady painting the fingernails of women and girls. That meant a lot to the girls. In Iraq, World Missions Alliance provided soccer balls, food for families, blankets, and space heaters.

Spiritual Tools

The sword is the Word of God, both the written and spoken Word. Repentance, praying in the Spirit, fasting, laying on hands, anointing, worship, and thanksgiving to God are effective in the spiritual dimension.

Special Operations Forces

Small Christian missionary teams are similar to special operations forces teams like the Navy SEALs. Members must have spiritual discipline. No sloppy physical, or spiritual, lifestyle will benefit the team. The team is as vulnerable as the weakest link allows. It is spiritual warfare. The mission is to gain ground and save lives and souls. You are a co-laborer with Christ; you are helping advance the Kingdom of God. Scripture says the Kingdom of God is righteousness, peace, and joy in the Holy Spirit. Love is key.

Force Multipliers

Special operations forces teams often have the goal to be *force multipliers.* They are to win the hearts and souls of the local people. When they win the hearts and souls of the local people for the Lord, they have multiplied their effort. Special operations forces teams also train and equip the indigenous forces. Now the local people are striving toward the same goals, bringing the Good News to others and expanding the Kingdom of God. They are, in effect, bringing Heaven to earth. Yeshua (Jesus) said to pray that God's will be done on earth as it is in Heaven. God's stated will is that none should perish, but that all would have everlasting life through Jesus.

Army Versus Special Operations Forces

I have heard sermons about how the function of the church is to occupy until the Lord returns. That is different than the function of missionaries. Armies occupy; the global church functions like an army. Missionaries, i.e., special operations forces, get in, get it done, and leave. Special operations forces have specific goals to accomplish. They have specific skills and equipment that they bring for the mission. There is a scheduled beginning and end to the mission.

The World Is a War Zone

Jesus said in Matthew 24 that nation will rise against nation and kingdom against kingdom. This world is a war zone. The kingdom of Satan is at war with the Kingdom of Heaven—perfect love versus despicable evil. In Matthew 16, Jesus says He "is building His Church and the Gates of Hades will not overcome it." The war began on Earth when Satan came to the garden of Eden to harm the first family. The war has continued until today. The prize is generations of souls of men, women, and children. This is a supernatural war not bound by natural laws of physics, biology, or chemistry—a spiritual war beyond the limits of science. A global international network of evil is being exposed. Daniel 11 says "the people that know their God shall be strong, and do exploits." God is on the move. He is the God of signs, wonders, and miracles. He has good works that He preordained for His people to do. Good is overcoming evil. Jesus is the Good Shepherd of Psalm 23. His sheep hear His voice (John 10:27).

What is God telling you?

Appendix

The following is a count of child predators who were in church or school leadership by state, per retired Texas appellate attorney Christa Brown, author of *This Little Light: Beyond a Baptist Preacher Predator and his Gang* (Foremost Press, 2009):

- Ralph Lee Aaron, Daniel Acker, Jr., Zachary Reed Emerson, Luis Federico Garcia, John Anderson, Benton Gray Harvey (Alabama)

- Tim Ballard (school principal), Keith Daniel Kiger, George "Tom" Wade, Travis Payne, David Pierce (Arkansas)

- Deacon Robert Harvey Alexander, Daniel Earl Allmond, Brian Brijbag, Lonnie Broome, Jim Kilburn Bruce, Jeffery Lamar Carter, Stephen Lee Edmonds, Jeremy Patrick Gable, Tommy Gilmore, Darrell Gilyard, Robert Gray, Jerry Hutcheson, Fritner Jean (Florida)

- Gordon H. Lunceford, Timothy Scott Richerson, Richard Frank Shaw, Nathan St. Pierre, Drew A. Underwood, John Brothers, Jr., Jacob Conder, Shawn Davies, John Wayne Diehl, (Kentucky)

- Robert M. Black, Mark Lewis Brooks, Joseph Edmond Conger, Michael Alan Crippen, Shawn Davies, George Hendon, Terry McDowell (Missouri)

- Sean David Whisenhunt, Billy Ray Smith, Joshua Spires, David Slone, Bruce Sanders, Emmett Hayslip, Doug Davis, Vincent Brookfield (Oklahoma);

- Donald Chrisler Batson, Stephen Douglas Berry, Gregory Martin Hill, John Hubner, Norman Henley Keesee, Marion Leon Kosier, Jr, Kevin Olge, (South Carolina)

- Joshua Allen, Dale (Dickie) Amyx, Andrew Argent, Matt Baker, Joe Barron, W. Frank Brown, Jerry Dale Carver, Ollin Collins, Sigifrido Flores, Shane Flournoy, Chad Foster, Gregory Charles Goben, Michael Lee Jones, Thomas Reid Jones, Joel Dean Joslin, Kevin Othell Laferney, John Langworthy, Stephen Livingston, Robert McClurg, John O. McKay, Billie Lewis Minson, Larry Nuell Neathery, Michael Wayne O'Guin, Joshua Neal Ponder, Larry Reynolds, Robert Riffle, Morris David Roberts, Frank Sizemore, Hezekiah Stallworth, Sam Underwood, Kenneth Ward, Robert John Weber, Charles "Rick" Willits (Texas)

BBC Articles Covering Child Abuse in the Church

The evidence is overwhelming that these are not individual personal vices. Related BBC articles include these:

"Ireland's hidden survivors" by Leanna Byrne, *BBC News* (https://www.bbc.co.uk/news/extra/BoWIe4x0Lj/Ireland_hidden_survivors).

"Sexual Abuse and the Catholic Church," from *America Magazine* (https://www.americamagazine.org/sexual-abuse-and-catholic-church).

"All Chile's 34 bishops offer resignation to Pope over sex abuse scandals," published by *BBC News* on May 18, 2018 (https://www.bbc.com/news/world-latin-america-44169484).

APPENDIX

"Police in Chile raid church offices during sex abuse investigation," published by the *Catholic News Agency* on June 14, 2018 (https://www. catholicnewsagency.com/news/police-in-chile-raid-church-offices-during-sex-abuse-investigation-74451). On the same day, *BBC News* published this article: "Chile police raid Catholic Church offices amid sex abuse scandal" (https://www.bbc.com/news/world-latin-america-44477890). The *BBC News* article reported that the government of Chile used their police force and special police to raid the church in an effort to gather evidence. It also reported that the Archbishop Charles Scicluna and MSGR Jordi Bertomeu had compiled a report that documents evidence of abuse cases covered up by the Chilean church. About 80 Roman Catholic priests have been reported to authorities in Chile for alleged sexual abuse over the last 18 years.

"Delhi Archdiocese Rejects Claims Of Sexual Abuse By Kerala Nun's Family," published by New Delhi Television Limited (NDTV) on July 10, 2018 (https://www.ndtv.com/india-news/delhi-archdiocese-rejects-claims-by-kerala-nuns-family-1880852).

"Abuse-concealing bishop to be held at home," YouTube video posted on August 14, 2018, by News 4 U (https://www.youtube.com/watch?time_continue=2&v=PMB8HySAPU8&feature=emb_logo).

"300 Pennsylvania Priests Accused of Child Sex Abuse—and One Got Reference for Disney World Job," by Dave Quinn, published August 15, 2018, by *People* (https://people.com/crime/pennsylvania-sex-abuse-report-catholic-church/).

"US priests abused thousands of children," by BBC Radio 4, posted on August 15, 2018 (https://www.bbc.co.uk/programmes/b0bf4cnr).

"Cardinal Cupich: Pope Should Not Resign Over Vigano Claims," posted August 27, 2018, on BBC's *Newshour* (https://www.bbc.co.uk/programmes/p06jlw26).

THE DOCTOR'S TRAVEL JOURNAL

"'Thousands' abused by German priests," on the BBC's *Global News Podcast*, September 12, 2018 (https://www.bbc.co.uk/programmes/p06l0lkk) *(recording no longer available)*.

Another article was titled "Chile abuse priest Fernando Karadima removed by Vatican" (https://www.bbc.com/news/world-middle-east-45677534). The article appeared on *BBC News* September 28, 2018. According to the article, Pope Francis removed the priest and said, "It was for the good of the church." The 88-year-old former priest who was previously sanctioned to a lifetime of "penance and prayer" for sexually abusing minors was now removed. In a Vatican investigation from 2011, Karadima was found guilty of abusing teenage boys over many years but he was not removed from the Vatican at that time and denies wrongdoing.

"US opens Catholic church sex abuse probe in Pennsylvania," published by *BBC News* on October 19, 2018 (https://www.bbc.com/news/world-us-canada-45909270).

"Spain child abuse: Victims fight back and appeal for change" by James Badcock, published on November 3, 2018 by *BBC News* (https://www.bbc.com/news/world-europe-46064017).

"Philip Wilson: Ex-archbishop's conviction for covering-up abuse is quashed," published on December 6, 2018 by *BBC News* (https://www.bbc.com/news/world-australia-46463771).

"Vatican abuse summit: Cardinal says files were destroyed," published on February 23, 2019 by *BBC News* (https://www.bbc.com/news/world-europe-47343458).

"Birmingham Archdiocese 'ignored abuse to protect reputation,'" published by *BBC News* on June 20, 2019 (https://www.bbc.com/news/uk-england-birmingham-48703484).

APPENDIX

"France's top cardinal guilty of sex abuse cover-up," published by DW on July 3, 2019 (https://www.dw.com/en/frances-top-cardinal-guilty-of-sex-abuse-cover-up/a-47804765).

"Polish abuse scandal: Victims take on Catholic Church," by Adam Easton, published by *BBC News* on July 22, 2019 (https://www.bbc.com/news/world-europe-49025423).

"Church sexual abuse: French priest Preynat admits 'caressing' boys," published by *BBC News* on January 14, 2020 (https://www.bbc.com/news/world-europe-51090077).

Patterns of activity are found in *BBC News* articles. These include the following:

"Paedophile jailed and body confidence mission" by Andrew Easton, *BBC Hereford & Worcester (episode no longer available)*. A man was convicted for 45 sex offences against young boys in England that could not be covered up.

"John Allen: Paedophile care home owner on trial for sex abuse," published on November 5, 2019 (https://www.bbc.com/news/uk-wales-50302873). John Allen ran a group of children's homes in England and abused many young boys for decades.

"The Gap Year Paedophile," posted on BBC One on March 7, 2018, covers similar offences against children in Malaysia (https://www.bbc.co.uk/programmes/p05gh2kb).

"Jeffrey Epstein: ABC stopped report 'amid Palace threats,'" published on November 5, 2019, by *BBC News*, shows connection of pedophile rings, the Royal family, and President Clinton and the cover-up (https://www.bbc.com/news/world-us-canada-50296742).

Related *BBC News* articles include these:

"US Labour Secretary Alex Acosta resigns over Epstein case" (https:// www.bbc.com/news/world-us-canada-48967419), published on July 12, 2019.

"Victoria's Secret boss 'embarrassed' by Jeffery Epstein ties" (https:// www.bbc.com/news/business-49653273), published on September 10, 2019.

"Prince Andrew's links to Jeffery Epstein" (https://www.bbc.com/ news/uk-49411215), published on November 16, 2019.

About the Author

Richard Paul Bartlett, M.D., has flown overseas to more than a dozen countries, volunteering with World Missions Alliance to provide medical care to those in need, in slums, refugee camps, and war zones. He has documented dangerous situations and narrow escapes in third-world and dictator-run countries. He has witnessed miraculous healing and irrefutable evidence of God's love while operating free medical clinics in tents, open fields, and the most pristine of conditions.

Dr. Bartlett has served as the medical director of multiple clinics, public and private ambulance services, nursing homes, emergency rooms, and a private hospital. He has served four terms as president of a county medical society. He has been the CBS News Medical Expert of West Texas for over 20 years and a regular guest medical contributor on KCRS 550 AM Talk Radio. He has served the Texas Medical Association on the Board of Councilors, Blood and Tissue Usage Committee, and the Council of Scientific Affairs. He served four terms as president of the county medical society.

He was appointed by the Texas governor to the newly formed Texas Health Disparities Taskforce. A two-year appointment, he was charged to advise the governor so that all Texans would have access to quality healthcare and due to yearly reappointments by the governor, he served a total of seven years. In appreciation of his contributions to the state of Texas, Dr. Bartlett was awarded the Meritorious Service Award from the Texas Health and Human Services Commissioner. He is the author of *Journey of a Medicine Man: Doctor Confirmed Miracles* (Emerge Publishing, 2018). He serves as the Medical Missions Director of World Missions Alliance.